BFI FILM CLASSICS
. . . .

Edward Buscombe
SERIES EDITOR

Colin MacCabe and David Meeker
SERIES CONSULTANTS

Cinema is a fragile medium. Many of the great classic films of the past now exist, if at all, in damaged or incomplete prints. Concerned about the deterioration in the physical state of our film heritage, the National Film and Television Archive, a Division of the British Film Institute, has compiled a list of 360 key films in the history of the cinema. The long-term goal of the Archive is to build a collection of perfect showprints of these films, which will then be screened regularly at the Museum of the Moving Image in London in a year-round repertory.

BFI Film Classics is a series of books commissioned to stand alongside these titles. Authors, including film critics and scholars, film-makers, novelists, historians and those distinguished in the arts, have been invited to write on a film of their choice, drawn from the Archive's list. Each volume presents the author's own insights into the chosen film, together with a brief production history and a detailed filmography, notes and bibliography. The numerous illustrations have been specially made from the Archive's own prints.

With new titles published each year, the BFI Film Classics series will rapidly grow into an authoritative and highly readable guide to the great films of world cinema.

Could scarcely be improved upon ... informative, intelligent, jargon-free companions.
The Observer

Cannily but elegantly packaged BFI Classics will make for a neat addition to the most discerning shelves.
New Statesman & Society

LES ENFANTS DU PARADIS

· · · · · · · · · · · · · · · · · · ·

Jill Forbes

BFI PUBLISHING

First published in 1997 by the
BRITISH FILM INSTITUTE
21 Stephen Street, London W1P 2LN

The British Film Institute exists
to promote appreciation, enjoyment, protection and
development of moving image culture in and throughout the
whole of the United Kingdom.
Its activities include the National Film and
Television Archive; the National Film Theatre;
the Museum of the Moving Image;
the London Film Festival; the production and
distribution of film and video; funding and support for
regional activities; Library and Information Services;
Stills, Posters and Designs; Research;
Publishing and Education; and the monthly
Sight and Sound magazine.

British Library Cataloguing-in-Publication Data
A catalogue record for this book is available from the British Library

ISBN 0–85170–365–8

Designed by
Andrew Barron & Collis Clements Associates

Typesetting by
D R Bungay Associates, Burghfield, Berks.

Printed in Great Britain

CONTENTS

à Claude Ramos

ACKNOWLEDGMENTS

I would like to record my thanks to the British Academy, the Carnegie Trust for the Universities of Scotland, and the University of Bristol, without whose generous financial support I could not have carried out the research for this book. I am also indebted to various friends and colleagues whose erudition illuminated aspects of French nineteenth-century history and culture, and in particular to Michael Freeman, Michael Kelly, Ed Lilley, Adrian Rifkin and Tony Sutcliffe. Parts of the book were read as papers at the Universities of Humberside, Leicester, Reading and Southampton and the resulting discussions did much to clarify my thinking about the film. In addition, I am grateful to the British Film Institute Stills, Posters and Designs Department. Finally, my thanks to Guy Rossi-Landi in whose delightful apartment, near the Batignolles, much of this was written.

A Note on Sources
Quotations from the script are taken from the edition published by Balland in 1974. All translations from the French are my own.

Othello murders Desdemona

INTRODUCTION

. . . .

Les Enfants du paradis is a work of incomparable richness and complexity, a deliberately playful text in which fiction and reality, film and theatre, are artfully intertwined and their boundaries confused. It is a film of immense scope and ambition, made at a crucial time in the history of France and of its cinema, which triumphantly surmounted all the constraints and restrictions of wartime, and which even today, half a century after it was first released, continues to be considered 'the greatest film ever made'.[1]

The gala première of *Les Enfants du paradis* was held at the Palais de Chaillot in Paris on 9 March 1945. The city had been liberated from German occupation for less than a year and the war was not yet over. But the streets were suddenly full of soldiers speaking English and the cinemas were screening long-banned American films. Many hopes were riding on *Les Enfants du paradis*. It was to be a showcase, a testimony to the French cinema's enduring qualities of imagination, and proof that it could stand up to foreign competition. For the director Marcel Carné the film represented the high point of his career; for the actors Arletty, Jean-Louis Barrault and Pierre Brasseur it was a professional watershed; for the set designer Alexandre Trauner it was his greatest achievement; and for the writer Jacques Prévert it was his last major contribution to the cinema. It was also a huge commercial success. Its first Paris run lasted for over a year and grossed 41 million francs.

The film would have been an impressive achievement under any circumstances, but under Occupation conditions it was little short of miraculous. Material shortages during the war made film-making a hazardous business. According to Carné, only the costumes for *Les Enfants du paradis* did not suffer from wartime restrictions. Procurement difficulties, unreliable transport, limits on the amount of film stock that could be used, and the regular power cuts, all made progress extremely laborious, as did rumours of Allied invasions. Often the crew worked for only an hour a day before being forced, by one shortage or another, to pack up. In these conditions, to undertake filming a spectacular lasting over three hours, requiring the largest and most complicated set ever built for a French film, and more than 1,500 extras, seems an extraordinary act of folly. Yet somehow 800 cubic metres of earth were shifted, 35 tonnes of scaffolding brought down from Paris, 300 tonnes of plaster and 500 square metres of glass were all found to recreate the nineteenth-century 'Boulevard du Crime'.[2]

Production started on 16 August 1943 at the Victorine Studios in Nice where the huge set was constructed. But the course of the war meant that the production had a chequered history. After only a few weeks, work was halted because of a rumour that the Americans had landed at Genoa. When Italy signed an armistice with the Allies in September 1943, the film's Italian co-producers withdrew and a hiatus of two months ensued. Carné and his team returned to Paris from Nice to find that the French producer of the film, André Paulvé, was under Nazi investigation and was pulling out. After further delay, Pathé agreed to take over the production which resumed on 9 November 1943 in their studios in Paris. The crew did not return to Nice until February 1944 by which time the set had been badly damaged by the weather and required further investment.

While the Nazis threatened Paulvé's business, the anti-semitic policies of the occupying forces and the Vichy government also caused difficulties. Neither the designer Alexandre Trauner, nor the composer Joseph Kosma, both of whom were Jews, could work on the film under their own names, so Léon Barsacq acted as a *prête-nom* for Trauner and Maurice Thiriet for Kosma. However, as the balance tipped towards an Allied victory, supporters of the Nazis began to run scared. Robert Le Vigan, the actor for whom the part of the old clothes-seller Jéricho was written, and who made many anti-semitic and pro-Nazi radio broadcasts during the war, fled in 1944 to join members of the Vichy government in the German town of Sigmaringen. Some controversy surrounds the number of scenes actually shot with Le Vigan as well as the date of his flight, but in the film as we have it today Jéricho is played by Pierre Renoir who was brought in as a last-minute substitute.

Despite all these vicissitudes, the production was nearing completion as the year 1944 drew to a close. But at this point Carné slowed proceedings down. The approaching end of the war opened up the possibility that instead of being the last film of the Occupation *Les Enfants du paradis* could be the first film of the Liberation. Chronologically, this is how things turned out. But as will become apparent, *Les Enfants du paradis* remains, in all other respects, a film of the Occupation years.

GENESIS OF THE FILM
. . . .

Les Enfants du paradis was allegedly born of a chance encounter which took place in the summer of 1942 between Jean-Louis Barrault, Marcel Carné and Jacques Prévert in a bar on the Promenade des Anglais in Nice. Barrault had come south for a holiday in St Tropez;[3] Prévert, like many of his compatriots, had abandoned Paris after the German invasion and had settled in the hills above Nice where he was hiding Trauner in his house; Carné, who was visiting, was in a state of depression because his latest film project had been turned down. Asked if he had any ideas for a film, Barrault proposed, 'the story of a mime artist and an actor, for example Deburau and Frédérick Lemaître'. The subject had much to recommend it to the various members of this group: Carné had an abiding ambition to make a 'great', spectacular film; Prévert had a longstanding interest in 'popular' Parisian culture; while Barrault, who was preoccupied with the need to revive the contemporary French theatre, saw it as a chance to exploit his research into theatre history and his work on mime.

But was the subject-matter appropriate? Film-makers who wished their projects to find favour with the censors had to navigate between the twin dangers of a German veto and Vichy's version of patriotism. Carné and Prévert's preceding film, *Les Visiteurs du soir* (1942), had successfully done this by recourse to a medieval setting reminiscent of one of the masterpieces of French Gothic art, *Les Très Riches Heures du Duc de Berry*. In fact, many films made under the Occupation similarly avoided the contemporary in favour of the historical, the fantastic, or what has been called the '*contemporain vague*'.[4] Credit sequences and opening shots often served to locate films somewhere other than France in the 1940s, a typical example, perhaps, being *Le Club des soupirants* whose credit sequence bears the legend 'Once upon a time in a happy country'.[5] With its action set in the 19th century, and in the world of theatre and entertainment, *Les Enfants du paradis* might hope to get past the censors with little difficulty. But does this setting mean that *Les Enfants du paradis* should be interpreted as an escapist fantasy with little or no relation to the sociopolitical context in which it was made? Or is it rather, as is frequently suggested, an allegory in which Arletty stands for the spirit of resistance and Nathalie compliance with the values of the Vichy regime? Or is it, perhaps, rooted in the Vichy experience in ways that are not as immediately obvious? In order to consider these questions properly we shall take a closer look at the conditions of film-making in occupied France.

AN ALTERNATIVE CULTURAL STRATEGY: THE FRENCH CINEMA UNDER THE OCCUPATION

It is no exaggeration to say that the Germans invaded France at a providential moment for the French film industry which had not recovered from the body-blow inflicted by the arrival of the talkies a decade earlier. Lack of investment had meant reliance on American or German technology, and by the late 1930s the two major production and distribution companies, Pathé and Gaumont, were technically bankrupt. The industry's problems were identified, in one of the many plans drawn up to rescue it, as lack of a central administration and professional organisation, the absence of adequate financing mechanisms, excessive taxation, and uncontrolled imports.

After they occupied the northern zone of France, the Germans adopted a dual policy towards the country's film industry, seeking to maintain film production, for propaganda purposes as well as to satisfy popular demand, but also attempting to colonise the French cinema so as to ensure that the German industry became pre-eminent in the new, Nazi-dominated Europe. Goebbels believed that to destroy what he saw as French cultural dominance in Europe, French film production should be merely 'local and limited'.[6] However, Alfred Greven, the former director of production at the UFA studios in Berlin, who was given overall responsibility for cinema in France, does not seem to have shared this view. Instead, he set about taking control of the French industry through the creation of a vertically integrated film empire, with his production company Continental Films, his distribution company ACE, his exhibition company SOGEC, and his studios and film-processing laboratories Paris-Studio-Cinéma. He achieved this by a series of purchases or injections of capital into existing companies, all of which were legal but would have been impossible had it not been for the flight and expropriation of many Jews who were prohibited from exercising certain trades and professions under Nazi laws. Greven also signed up as many French directors as possible to work for his new company. Although independent French producers were allowed to continue operations, Continental Films was always top of the pile when it came to supplies of film stock, building materials, studio space or electricity. Working for Greven was therefore attractive, and by the end of the war, his company had produced nearly 15 per cent of all films made in France (more than any other single producer) and had employed such popular and distinguished directors as Cayatte, Clouzot and Decoin. Carné himself was briefly contracted to Greven in 1941 before managing to find an excuse to break his agreement.

There seems little doubt that Greven's entrepreneurial activities, and the threat of artistic competition they posed, galvanised the French industry, or what remained of it, into the creation of institutional and administrative structures, based on state support and a powerful trade organisation. The civil servant Guy de Carmoy was now able to implement a rescue plan for the industry drawn up in 1936, with the result that during the German occupation, the French film industry became more successful than it had been for a very long time.[7] Measures such as the incorporation of all technicians into a single craft organisation facilitated the identification of 'Jews and foreigners', who were then excluded from working by the racial laws enacted both by the occupying forces and the Vichy regime. But they also stimulated the careers of many aspiring film-makers who had found it hard to make a living in the stagnant conditions of the industry in the 1930s. For although nearly 50 per cent of film-makers and actors left France – among them Renoir, Duvivier, Feyder and Clair, Jouvet, Gabin and Michèle Morgan – many others, such as Bresson, Becker and Clouzot, benefited from the career opportunities provided by the war. Carné, who was already a well-established director, found that circumstances promoted him to the first rank and gave him the chance to make ambitious films that he might not have been offered in peacetime. The views expressed by Marcel L'Herbier when he came to write his memoirs in 1979 could be used to sum up what many film-makers felt about the German occupation at the time: 'For the most part we film directors had been working in an atmosphere of artistic slavery since 1930, even though France was then free. Now that it no longer was, and the Germans had the whip hand, the situation was completely reversed and we regained the right to complete artistic freedom.'[8]

Carmoy's major concern was that the French film industry should remain in French hands and should flourish in the new Europe. In addition to conducting protracted negotiations over the industry in the Occupied Zone, he therefore turned his attention to the south coast and its production facilities.[9] The idea that a 'French Hollywood' should be established on the Côte d'Azur had received considerable discussion during the period immediately preceeding the war. Marcel L'Herbier actively promoted the idea.[10] Renoir, for his part, wrote a report in which he suggested the establishment of a 'cinema city' in Nice, capitalising on the climate and existing infrastructure to create a sort of ideal artistic community bringing together directors, writers, actors and designers, and providing apprenticeships and training for those wishing to enter the business. A stimulus of this kind was badly needed for the Nice studios had languished since the advent of the talkies, and of the six that had existed in the silent period only two, the Victorine and those at St-Laurent-du-Var, were still functioning in 1940, the former being by far the larger and better equipped, with seven shooting stages and space for building sets.

In order to prevent German capital seizing control of production capacity in the south as well as in the north, Carmoy intervened to ensure that the lease on the Victorine Studios should be sold to the French company SESCA, whose chairman was the producer André Paulvé. Carmoy also encouraged Paulvé to enter into partnership with the Italians as a bulwark against the Germans, the Italians having, in any case, geopolitical ambitions in the Nice region. Paulvé's interests were undoubtedly promoted because he had been engaged in Italian co-productions since 1939, and because he was one of the entrepreneurs who managed to expand his operations during the war. Moreover, his Italian connexions served him in good stead with regard to the rationing of materials, power and screens in the Occupied Zone where Italian, or Franco-Italian companies came second only to Continental Films in the pecking order for allocations.[11] Thus in 1942, with the approval of both the French and Italian governments, the newly created CIMEX company, backed by 60 per cent Italian capital and 40 per cent French (Paulvé's), and with Paulvé as managing director, rented the Victorine Studios and produced some of the best-known films of the period, *Les Enfants du paradis* among them.[12]

Les Enfants du paradis was an integral part of Paulvé's commercial strategy. From 1938 when he first entered the film business in partnership with Adolphe Osso, Paulvé had rapidly become one of the most important producers and distributors of French films and his catalogue included Carné's *Le Quai des brumes*, Grémillon's *Lumière d'été* and Delannoy's *L'Eternel Retour*. In a career that continued into the 1960s, he also produced Cocteau, L'Herbier, Becker and Clément. He was therefore well placed to support ambitious projects and was far from daunted by the scope of Carné and Prévert's pretentions. In *Les Visiteurs du soir*, he had financed an expensive historical reconstruction which had been a huge commercial and artistic success, and was therefore both willing and able to reinvest in the Carné team. And he undoubtedly saw *Les Enfants du paradis* as a useful exploitation of the resources of the Victorine and its workers, since the studio, as is affectionately recalled in Truffaut's *La Nuit américaine*, was famous for its large sets.

The strategy of promoting Nice as an alternative film production venue to Paris was very successful, and, by 1941, nine films, employing an estimated 400 people, were in production (as against only thirty shot in Nice between 1930 and 1940).[13] In this way, the Victorine became the focus of Vichy's alternative cultural strategy which was based on the production of authentically French films, made by French technicians, in French-controlled studios. *Les Visiteurs du soir*, the box-office hit of 1942, was a prime example of this new approach: contemporary critics saw it as utterly different from anything produced by Hollywood, and praised it as a cinematic reinterpretation of one of the monuments of French art for which the best resources – director, writer, designers, actors – of the French cinema had been mobilised.[14] In a climate where anti-Americanism and narrow patriotism reigned, a repeat of this kind of success would be welcome. Once again L'Herbier spoke for the profession in an interview with a Nice newspaper in 1940, describing not just the ambition to get

> the film industry going again on the Côte d'Azur, [but] a much greater undertaking which looks towards the future and is more in tune with what France expects in order to support its revival and the influence of its cinema. A national, and in due course European, industrial and artistic film production centre must be created on the Mediterranean coast.[15]

One of the most significant meanings of *Les Enfants du paradis* is that it contributes to a nationalist project. It is a work which was designed to

Trauner's set of the Boulevard du Temple

fulfil the ambition, nourished by film-makers, Vichy sympathisers and French patriots alike, to beat the Americans at their own game by producing a spectacular film which was distinctively French. Its scale and ambition were marks of the vitality of French culture, politically important statements that French individuality would survive assaults, both from elsewhere in Europe and from across the Atlantic.

HISTORY AND FICTION

Les Enfants du paradis is presented as a historical reconstruction in which the setting, characters and events depicted for the most part really existed. Indeed, much of our pleasure as viewers derives from the sense of authenticity procured by the film, a sense which director and set designer were at great pains to achieve. At the same time, the film promotes an ambiguous relationship between history and fiction by blurring chronology and the passage of time, by introducing characters for whom no historical source exists and, more generally, by leading the viewer into a world committed to total unreality, to fantasy, pretence, disguise and make-believe, the world of nineteenth-century theatre and entertainment.

The exact date of the setting is difficult to pinpoint, but some fascinating clues are offered. According to Carné, the 'action takes place round 1840'.[16] On the other hand, the script published by *L'Avant-scène cinéma* states 'we are in 1827 or 1828, the precise date does not matter',[17] while on some copies of the film (often those shown abroad), but not the one transcribed for publication,[18] the date of 1830 is given at the beginning of the first part of the film. In addition, the film is divided into two parts or 'periods', between which six years elapse, the characters age, and their social circumstances change. It appears certain, therefore, that the film is set in the period of the July Monarchy, that is between 1830 and 1848, for the latter is the date at which the fairs on the Boulevard du Temple, of the kind seen right at the end of the film, ceased to be held. The action must also have taken place before 1862 when the Théâtre des Funambules was destroyed by fire.

Precise dating is not just avoided, however, but perhaps deliberately confused. There is, for example, no reference to political events – the two revolutions that brought into being and terminated the

July Monarchy are notably absent – while certain characters, events and settings appear to bear more relation to the Paris of the Belle Epoque than to that of the 1830s.[19] In fact, the 'real' events in *Les Enfants du paradis*, that is, the events which can be documented from historical sources, do not belong to politics at all but to art and literature, to the history of the theatre and of entertainment, and especially the traditions of the French Romantic theatre.

The set of *Les Enfants du paradis* is the principle means by which a sense of authenticity is created and by which we are convinced the film is a historical reconstruction. It was the largest and most elaborate to have been built in a French studio, and the crowning achievement of Alexandre Trauner's career.[20] Its size and magnificence were clearly intended as a way of showing the world what France could do even when the odds were stacked against her, an act of defiance against the Germans and, more distantly, Hollywood. The set frames the two halves of the film, generating the actors at the beginning and swallowing them up at the end, becoming, as Carné was to emphasise in his autobiography, a significant actor in the film.[21]

The major exterior set in the film is the reconstruction of the Boulevard du Temple which in the 19th century developed as a theatre location because of an already existing tradition of popular entertainment and promenading. The Boulevard had been laid out in the middle of 17th century, and after it was planted with trees at the beginning of the 18th century it became a favourite place for idle strolling, or *flânerie*. The crowds attracted all kinds of individuals selling their wares; cake shops, cafés and *cabarets* (drinking houses) were established; and travelling entertainers came to perform along the Boulevard.[22] As this was for centuries the city wall and thus free from the need for Royal privilege (or licence), it was the place where theatres were constructed, so as to remain as close as possible to potential audiences.[23] To judge from the nineteenth-century prints and engravings that inspired the sets of *Les Enfants du paradis* we can see that this 'fairground' tradition had not disappeared with the construction of the theatres. Instead, various forms of entertainment, both indoor and outdoor, existed side by side, catering to many different tastes and pockets, with the most popular at the south-eastern end of the Boulevard, nearest to the Bastille, and the most aristocratic at the north-western end, nearest to the present-day Opéra Garnier.[24]

Carné and Trauner went to great lengths to achieve a sense of authenticity. Carné collected photographs of prints and engravings from the Bibliothèque Nationale, the Musée Carnavalet and other Paris archives of the history of the city, and brought them to the designer's hideout in the Mediterranean. Trauner's design technique was influenced by his apprenticeship to Lazare Meerson, a Russian designer who had emigrated to Paris in the 1930s where he had become head of a permanent team of set designers based at the Epinay Studios. Meerson had created the vogue for elaborate sets and period reconstructions, and both Carné and Trauner had worked on one of his most spectacular efforts, *La Kermesse héroïque* (1935), which has obvious affinities with Carné's masterpiece in its re-creation of the spirit of carnival in a sixteenth-century fair in Flanders, and its debate about resistance to invasion and collaboration with occupying forces.

Trauner recalled how he followed Meerson in detesting 'primary realism',[25] relying instead, as he had done for his composite re-creation of Victorian/Edwardian London in Carné's *Drôle de drame*, on the sources offered by contemporary illustrations, which are 'already selections of reality'. 'I always look at them very closely because they show me what I

must use. They are a necessary crutch to enable us to identify the elements that will be recognised by people watching the film.'[26] In this way the sets were intended to carry a powerful emotional charge deriving from the reconstruction or visualisation of artistic and cultural memories of places which, in many cases, no longer existed – at least in their nineteenth-century form. The charm of Trauner's sets is the charm of recognition, the pleasure deriving from the fact that the physical environment is exactly as the viewer somehow always expected it to be, a second-level re-creation based on the impressions of other artists and illustrators already in wide circulation. Paradoxically, the success of the sets derives from their lack of inventiveness and from their conformity to an ideal 'original' which we already carry in our mind's eye. One of Trauner's specialisms (following Meerson) was the trompe l'œil which is used in the crowd scenes of the film on the Boulevard du Temple where the last twenty metres of the set were painted, and child extras were brought in to increase the sense of perspective. The technique serves to enhance the exemplarity of the Boulevard, which is depicted as longer, more crowded and more lively than reality. It thus heightens the Boulevard's utopian quality, so that it resembles a memory enhanced and embellished by time,

'Truth' shoulder deep

in the manner of childhood memories, slightly larger (or longer) than life because dragged up from the recesses of our unconscious. In this way the set represents Paris in the 19th century not necessarily as it was, but as we wish to remember it having been.

Les Enfants du paradis focuses on the different kinds of entertainments strung out along what had become known as – because of the bloody plots of the melodramas regularly performed in its various theatres – the 'Boulevard du Crime'. Indeed, as the film opens, the camera behaves rather like a passer-by strolling along the Boulevard du Temple, drawn by turns to the different attractions along the way, and tempted to inspect them more closely. First we encounter a tightrope walker, a performing monkey and a weightlifter. Then what seems to be a purely fairground attraction, 'Truth', in the person of Arletty, displayed in a barrel inside a tent which, for a few sous, the curious passer-by can inspect. Then come the various theatres which all experienced days of fame on the Boulevard: the Ambigu-Comique, built in 1789, where Frédérick Lemaître scored a hit in *L'Auberge des Adrets* and which moved in 1827 to the Boulevard St Martin; the Folies Dramatiques, opened in January 1831, where in 1835 Lemaître scored another hit in *Robert Macaire*; the Théâtre des Funambules, opened in 1816 (and burnt down in 1862), which could seat over seven hundred people, and where the cheapest seats cost only 25 centimes. It specialised in pantomimes, and between 1825, or thereabouts, and 1846, when he died, the theatre employed the 'clown' or mime artist Jean-Baptiste Debureau (sometimes spelt 'Deburau') on whom the character of Baptiste is based. We see the young Baptiste sitting outside the theatre while his father attempts to whip up an audience for the show. After Debureau became famous, a huge model of a clown was affixed to the façade of the Funambules leaning out over the the Boulevard, and this we also see at a later point in the film.

Contemporary illustrations also show the numerous *cabarets* strung out along the Boulevard, among which figure Aux Lionceaux du Temple and L'Epi scié, and some of the characters who throng the street, notably the old clothes-seller, [Mar]Chand d'habits, whose dress is faithfully reproduced from a nineteenth-century print. There, however, one important venue shown in the set of the Boulevard du Temple which does not seem to be historically attested, and this is the Turkish baths in which Lacenaire murders the Comte de Montray. There was an oriental tea garden on the Boulevard, at about the point where the baths are situated, but the baths themselves are an invention which Trauner attributed to memories of such establishments in the Budapest of his childhood. Similar baths are to be found in films with orientalist themes that he designed later in his career such as Orson Welles's *Othello* (1950) which has obvious links with *Les Enfants du paradis* and Arthur Joffé's *Harem* (1985), but the invented baths here also have a thematic function, as we shall see.

Turning away from the Boulevard itself, we encounter another set for which there is a historical source. This is the Barrière de Ménilmontant seen when Baptiste and Garance are standing on the city wall looking out over the lights twinkling in the distance. The *'mur des fermiers généraux'*, a customs wall facilitating the collection of tolls and taxes on goods in transit, was erected in 1784 and not demolished until 1860, at which point it was used as the foundation for the construction of concentric boulevards within the city, and it is from this vantage point that Garance and Baptiste contemplate the lights.

The Barrière de Ménilmontant was one of a number of 'bars', or crossing points through the wall, where customs houses were erected,

Vendors on the Boulevard: a nineteenth-century view
(Photothèque des Musées de la Ville de Paris © DACS 1997)

many of them on the neoclassical lines which are meticulously reproduced in the film. But it also marked the point beyond which the city's juridisdiction did not extend, and hence the place where *cabarets* were set up to sell the '*vin de la barrière*', or tax-free wine.[27] The space, '*la zone*', beyond the wall was viewed as a wild area peopled by bandits and assorted outlaws, '*mauvais garçons*' and prostitutes known as 'Vénus de la barrière', a place not only in which the writ of the law did not run, but where the normal conventions of civilised society did not obtain. This is no doubt why the Rouge-gorge, the tavern sited *extra muros*, to which Bapiste's nocturnal wanderings take him, has a name whose macabre implications (red-breast/red-throat) Fil de soie and Lacenaire both underline with their cut-throat gestures.

The use of this setting has particular symbolic significance. The *barrières* themselves were often the site of symbolic or ritual acts, especially the Barrière St Jacques, where the gibbet was erected, whose tradition of grim associations are described at some length by Victor Hugo in *Le Dernier Jour d'un condamné* and *Les Misérables*. However, the *barrières* were also the places where barriers dropped, where aristocrats, bourgeois and working class mingled in a way that was

The Barrière de Ménilmontant in the 19th century
(Photothèque des Musées de la Ville de Paris © DACS 1997)

unthinkable elsewhere, and experienced together things that they would normally have experienced separately if at all.[28] Here thieves, prostitutes and all other individuals who easily crossed class barriers abounded. Here it was possible to 'go over to the other side' and to become something else. This was both a geographical and social fact and a literary trope: Baptiste's conversation with the blind beggar, Fil de soie, who leans against the city wall to accost passers-by, but who miraculously regains his sight once inside the Rouge-gorge, makes use of a commonplace of popular literature, the thieves' kitchen or *cour des miracles* found in *The Beggar's Opera*, in Victor Hugo's *Notre-Dame de Paris*, and in a series of Expressionist films such as Pabst's *Threepenny Opera* (after Brecht) which Carné saw and admired. At the *barrière*, truth is frequently the opposite of appearance, things are never quite what they seem, and are always susceptible of transformation: it is, as Fil de soie makes clear, a physical and metaphorical place of transgression.

But the reference to Ménilmontant serves to add another chrono-logical and artistic dimension to the historical framework of the film. For Ménilmontant as a symbolic locus is a *fin de siècle* rather than a July Monarchy creation, the place from which the decent, heroic working

Garance and Baptiste at the Barrière

class emerged into mythical status in material such as Aristide Bruant's song 'Ménilmontant'. Indeed, as Adrian Rifkin has remarked, the Ménilmontant Garance points out to Baptiste is a perfect anachronism since the sparsely populated village would hardly have glowed so brightly on the horizon in the 1830s, unlike its neighbour Belleville.[29] Moreover, the vantage point from which Garance and Baptiste look out is a '*montmartrois*' viewpoint, immortalised, for example, by Maurice Chevalier in his song 'Ménilmuche'. Ménilmontant is that lost innocence of working class decency and purity, left behind by Garance, along with her happiness, when she left her mother's house and came to the big city. Like Zola's Nana, Garance's mother was a laundress,[30] but, like Nana, Garance herself has opted to go over to the other side, and her act on the Boulevard du Crime is only the first of the series of transformations she will undergo in the film.

In this way, the anachronistic reference to Ménilmontant allows the film to enter a world different from that of pure historical reconstruction, to recall both the Montmartre culture of the turn of the century and all the debates which raged throughout the 1920s and 1930s about the modernisation of Paris, the destruction of '*les fortifs*' (a second ring of fortifications round Paris), and the cleansing of '*la zone*' beyond it.[31] Wherever the barriers are placed, whether on the *mur* or the *fortifs*, it is the area beyond, paradise of rag-and-bone men and dealers in junk – today the site of fleamarkets – that serves to define and enclose the essential and quintessential city.[32] By pointing outside, and turning her back on the area outside the city, Garance confirms the extent to which she, Baptiste and all the other characters in the film, are an artistic construction, committed denizens of an imagined world in which people invent their own identities to fit the setting in which they find themselves.

CARNÉ, BARRAULT, PRÉVERT –
LES VÉRITABLES AUTEURS DU CRIME

Carné's success as a film-maker was in part due to the fact that he always worked with the same small team: the writer Jacques Prévert (except for *Hôtel du nord*), the set designer Alexandre Trauner (except for *Jenny*) and the composers Joseph Kosma and Maurice Jaubert. He also tended to use the same small group of actors: Jean-Louis Barrault, Louis Jouvet,

Jean Gabin, Arletty and Pierre Brasseur. Jaubert was killed in 1940; Jouvet and Gabin were absent from France for the duration of the war; but the remainder of the 'team' were all present on *Les Enfants du paradis*. Carné's preferred method of work was closer to that of the Hollywood studio than to the auteurist approach which we now associate with French cinema. In addition to working within a group, his attention to detail and his perfectionism, his use of an elaborate storyboard and extensive rehearsals, and his capacity to organise large groups of people in complicated and lengthy shots (an ability which is magnificently displayed in *Les Enfants du paradis*), all point to the extent to which Carné saw himself as the conductor of a large orchestra, the master of a grand style reminiscent of D. W. Griffith at his most flamboyant. This, of course, was one of the reasons Carné was so successful during the war years, when film stock and electricity were rationed out by the Germans on the basis of a storyboard which meant that no one could afford to change their mind or make mistakes.

However, *Les Enfants du paradis* was not just a team effort in the sense that it was made in accordance with the production values typical of the large studios, it was also a compendium of the personal interests and preoccupations of its three principal originators, Carné, Barrault and Prévert. The plot they hatched in their discussions in the south of France was a bold attempt to offer a conspectus of their various interests in popular entertainment as represented in painting, theatre, literature and the cinema, so that the origins and meaning of *Les Enfants du paradis* are to be found, in part, in the earlier careers of each of its three creators which all contributed significantly to the final shape of the film.

Carné embarked on his career as a film-maker with a short documentary he financed himself entitled *Nogent, Eldorado du dimanche* (1929). In the early 1930s he worked as assistant to René Clair on *Sous les toits de Paris* (1930) and to Jacques Feyder on *Le Grand Jeu* (1933), *Pension Mimosas* (1934) and *La Kermesse héroïque* (1935). He cast Feyder's wife, Françoise Rosay, in the leading role in his first feature *Jenny* (1936) in which, as the mature, worldly-wise woman disappointed in love, she played an early avatar of Garance, as well as in *Drôle de drame* (1937) where her comic love scene with Jean-Louis Barrault is a model for that between Arletty and Barrault in *Les Enfants du paradis*. There followed *Hôtel du nord* (1938), and the masterpieces of poetic realism, *Le Quai des brumes* (1938) and *Le Jour se lève* (1939). When the war came Carné spent a brief period under contract to Alfred Greven at Continental Films before embarking on *Les Visiteurs du soir* (1942), and he devoted the remainder of the war to *Les Enfants du paradis* which, despite its period setting, reveals many continuities of subject, character, plot and narrative with his earlier work.

Carné acknowledged two main influences which are of particular relevance here. The first is the painting of the Impressionists about whom he was still attempting to make a film as late as 1991. Indeed, as a native of the Batignolles area of northern Paris, Carné may well feel a particular sympathy for Manet, Renoir and other members of the École des Batignolles who, in the 1860s and 1870s, had studios in this district of Paris. Impressionist painting undoubtedly influenced Carné because it represented a new realism, the poetry of the ordinary and what Baudelaire called the heroism of modern life, with the result that reminiscences of the Impressionist school abound in the topography of his films, their cast of characters, and the milieux they depict.

Many of the preferred locations of Impressionist painting are contained within an arc that can be described from west to east, from the newly developed boulevards in the west, with their ironwork balconies and imposing façades, across the Batignolles and Montmartre to Barbès, the Gare du Nord and the Canal St Martin, taking in the Boulevard de Clichy with its cabarets and prostitutes, home of the Moulin Rouge and the Folies Bergères, and the great railway terminus of the Gare St Lazare, subject of Monet's celebrated series of canvases. Carné recalls the Impressionists' depiction of these districts in the panoramic opening shot of *Les Portes de la nuit* (1946) which sweeps across the rooftops of the northern areas of the city in a manner reminiscent of the typical Impressionist 'point of view' – '*la vue plongeante*' or high shot – exemplified in paintings such as Monet's *La Fête, rue Montorgueil*,[33] as well as in *Les Enfants du paradis* where it is used most notably in the closing shots of the carnival on the Boulevard du Temple and evoked as a memory by Garance's gesture towards Ménilmontant when she is standing at the *barrière*.

In the same way, the population of working-class women (shop girls, flower sellers, dancers), *demi-mondaines* and prostitutes, and the new urban landscape of railways stations, parks and cafés, or the new leisure activities, such as boating and swimming in the Seine or the Marne, or drinking and dancing in a riverside *guinguette* (open-air dance hall) are Impressionist subjects deliberately recalled in Carné's films. Thus the milieu of prostitution and *demi-mondaines* is to be found in *Jenny*, *Hôtel du nord* and *Le Jour se lève*. Jenny is an *entremetteuse* who organises '*rencontres mondaines*', using as a front a lingerie boutique situated in the rue de Paradis. Clara in *Le Jour se lève* is a dancer and a girl of easy virtue while Madame Raymonde in *Hôtel du nord* is a streetwalker. Both the latter roles were played by Arletty who had therefore acquired a reputation for playing prostitutes in her career before *Les Enfants du paradis*. The world of entertainment and leisure is represented in *Jenny* and *Le Jour se lève*, while the modern forms of transport, and the architecture they inspired, figure in the barges passing through the lock on the Quai de Jemmapes in *Hôtel du nord*, the docks of Le Havre in *Le Quai des brumes*, the overhead métro in *Les Portes de la nuit*, while *Hôtel du nord* contains a fascinating shot of the Pont de l'Europe, subject of one of Caillebotte's best-known canvases, but in Carné's film enveloped in steam in a shot that is imitated from King Vidor's *The Crowd* (1928). Well before *Les Enfants du paradis*, which is of course entirely set in the world of entertainment and leisure, Carné had established these *topoi* as central to the modernity his films depict.

However, where Impressionist paintings appear to celebrate a new freedom of movement and the exuberance of popular leisure, Carné's films often turn on the dialectic of imprisonment and freedom, and his characters frequently evoke their desire 'to get away from it all'. Many of them, one way or the other, are on the run but cannot escape, for whatever reason, or if they have done so, they are irresistibly drawn to return. The entire action of *Les Enfants du paradis* apparently takes place in the enclosed space of a stage, and although Garance dreams of leaving in Part One, and by Part Two has been to India and spent long years in Scotland, she inevitably and irresistibly returns to her old Parisian haunts even though they amount to a form of imprisonment in what Lacenaire calls a gilded cage.

The tone of Carné's films also seems far removed from that of Impressionist paintings. His pleasures always seem touched with melancholy. His characters speak endlessly about starting afresh in the Paradise to which they propose to transport themselves, but the trains and railway stations which, under Monet's brush, are transformed by steam into symphonies of colour and plays of light and shade, serve in Carné's films to suggest a profound sadness, while in *Hôtel du nord* and

Le Jour se lève, the steam from trains is linked with suicide and self-immolation. The only way the characters achieve escape is through dance which is perhaps more central to Carné's pre-1946 cinema than any other activity. Whether it be *kermesse*, *bal populaire*, formal *gavotte* or a couple waltzing alone, it is the dance which procures the physically induced transport that allows the characters to remain where they are while imagining themselves elsewhere. The formal patterns, the changing configurations of bodies within an enclosed space, give rise to Carné's most flamboyant displays of directorial virtuosity in *Les Enfants du paradis*. They are prefigured in the *bal populaire* in the Rouge-gorge tavern in Part One, when we first hear the music of the carnival scene, and they are magisterially executed in the closing moments of the film when, accompanied by the same music which has now become much louder, the brightly lit Boulevard du Crime is filled with crowds dressed like clowns who are hideous parodies of Baptiste's most famous act, and whose riotous festivity swallows up the mime artist. It is the perfect figure for the dialectic of freedom and constraint which underpins Carné's aesthetic, the simultaneous ecstasy and misery of the carnival scene, the paradise from which Baptiste can never escape.

In using some of the *topoi* of Impressionism in a film ostensibly set at an earlier period but made in a later period, Carné not only inhibits precise dating, as has already been suggested, but also posits a counter-tradition of popular representation which runs from the theatre at the beginning of the 19th century to the cinema in the middle of the 20th and which is summed up in the title of the film. He also shows how the cinema inherited from Impressionist painting the task of representing the city and its inhabitants.

It is perhaps no accident that the directors Carné worked for, such as Clair and Feyder, and the American and German film-makers whose works he explored in the articles he published in *Cinémagazine* in the late 1920s and 1930s, all transform the modern city into an actor in the drama, and that Expressionist film-making was a second crucial influence on him. From these mentors Carné learned how to explore the visual possibilities of light and shadow, to exploit architectural features and industrial structures that form interesting shapes and patterns, and to treat the human face and body as elements in a larger, more abstract design. He has a predilection for locations such as the Pont de l'Europe or the Pont St Martin with their intricate ironwork, for ships' masts, and for docks with their jumble of cranes often wreathed in mist, for prison grilles and, quintessentially, for that masterpiece of ironwork the Barbès-Rochechouart métro station which is the setting of *Les Portes de la nuit*. But he also films the human body so as to render it more abstract and incorporate it into the urban environment.

Carné wrote two articles for *Cinémagazine* which go some way towards explaining how he conceived the function of the cinema and what he sought in *Les Enfants du paradis*. In 'La Caméra personnage du drame' (The camera as character in the play), written in 1929, he discusses Murnau's use of the tracking shot, a technical advance which Carné believed transformed the psychology of the cinema, changing the relationship between actors and space, allowing them to be, as it were, surprised in their environment by the inquisitive camera. This lesson is put to good effect in the opening sequence of *Les Enfants du paradis* and in the series of 'revelations' throughout the film, which allow the spectator to embark on a journey of discovery, peering through the 'keyhole of life'.[34]

In 'Quand le cinéma descendra-t-il dans la rue?' (When will the cinema go out into the street?) Carné investigates how sound cinema, by forcing film-making off the streets and into the studios, has deprived film of its capacity to record reality, and divorced it from its roots in popular entertainment by persuading it to imitate the bourgeois theatre in its dialogue and *mise en scène*. This is why *Les Enfants du paradis* is profoundly nostalgic for the freedom of the silent cinema whose aesthetics are constantly evoked in the film's emphasis on gesture and mime. In this article the capacity to film the city and its people is posited as the touchstone of cinema as a popular art, and set design is seen as the means by which cinema retained that capacity in the era of sound. In this way, the set serves not merely as a substitute for authentic locations but as a form of superior reality and a means of discovery so that

> one day when strolling round the outer districts of Paris we could swear we suddenly came across the streets invented by Meerson [whose] startling authenticity we find so moving – perhaps more moving than if [the film crew] had actually taken themselves off to the real scene of the action.

The manner of representing these sites is as important as the fact that they are represented. In the early part of the 19th century the combined effects of political and industrial revolution had swept away what has been called the 'transparent semiotics of the ancien régime' and destroyed the immediate legibility of the city and the people in it. Illuminated panoramas sought to restore that legibility in an attempt to display the city to the popular gaze so as to dispel the mystery and the menace of an environment which had become incomprehensible and oppressive.[35] They are recalled as precursors of the cinema in Garance's nostalgic gesture towards the world she has lost or left behind at the Barrière de

ANG

THEATRE LYRIQUE   CAFÉ DE L'ÉPI SCIE   ANCIEN CIRQUE

BOULEVARD D

Ménilmontant and in the long shots of the Boulevard du crime with its deliberately heightened perspective and strong lighting.

Such popular representations contrast with the hierarchised and ordered images of academic painting and drawing, and this is especially the case of the set of the Boulevard du Crime. If it is compared with the visual sources consulted by Carné and Trauner we can see that there are quite significant differences. The nineteenth-century prints and engravings show an open and spacious boulevard on which the buildings

ARIS

Editeur MOULINET, Peinture, 22, Rue du Temple, Paris

DRAMATIQUES   THÉATRE DE LA GAITÉ   FUNAMBULES DÉLASS^{ts}-COMIQUES LAZARI

MPLE (Démoli en 1862)

are set out in neatly spaced order, whereas Trauner's set depicts a jumble of tightly packed neoclassical facades and strongly pitched gables which are filmed at an oblique angle so as to emphasise their lack of classical proportions and the play of light and shade. Both images are to some degree imaginary. The nineteenth-century representations sought to achieve an ideal harmony which was to some extent realised in Haussmann's perspectives and uniform façades. In the inter-war years immediately preceeding the making of the film, there was a similar belief that rationalisation through architecture would overcome disorder and distortion, and would be able to 'clean up' the outlying areas so as to render them amenable to development and expansion.[36] By contrast, the set of *Les Enfants du paradis* recreates the sites of popular entertainment in the Rouge-gorge and on the Boulevard du Crime and, like the low-life literature of the 19th century, celebrates the culture of '*la zone*', and the disorder and vitality of a city still owned and lived in by the people, a city that has not yet fallen prey to scientific capitalism, which retains a human face and human dimensions, and which, thanks to cinema, remains within the comprehension of the ordinary gaze.

Jean-Louis Barrault and the Body
The second crucial member of Carné's team was Jean-Louis Barrault, who apparently had the original idea for *Les Enfants du paradis*, and who plays the centrally important role of the mime Baptiste, a performance of such virtuosity and pathos that it is often what audiences remember best from the film. Barrault's interest in the art of mime dated back to his apprenticeship with Charles Dullin and his friendship, in the 1930s, with Etienne Decroux, cast here in the role of Baptiste's father Anselme Debureau. (This friendship later soured, which may be why, in the film, relations between father and son are poor.) Together, they studied mime, with a view to exploring the way the actor can use the physical resources of the body, developing the famous illusionist technique of walking on the spot performed here by Baptiste in the pantomime *Les Amoureux de la lune*. Barrault's interest in nineteenth-century mime was related to his view of theatre history and the impact that the famous mime artist was said (by contemporary critics such as Janin and Gautier) to have had in expanding its repertoire and resources and in changing acting styles.

Another source of inspiration was the Russian theatre, particularly as developed by Vsevelod Meyerhold in the first decades of the century.[37]

Like Prévert and, indeed, like many French writers and artists, Barrault was attracted by the ferment of experimentation in Russia and the Soviet Union before and immediately after the 1917 Revolution. Meyerhold's emphasis on the 'theatre of the mask' and 'the idea of acting based on the apotheosis of the mask, gesture and movement [which] is indivisible from the idea of a travelling show'[38] was one which had obvious affinities with his own interest in using the resources of the body and his researches in technique and style. Meyerhold's notion of the 'cabotin' (he uses the French word) prefigures what Dullin and Barrault attempted to do in the 1930s: 'Is a theatre without cabotinage possible?', wrote Meyerhold. 'The cabotin is a strolling player; the cabotin is kinsman to the mime, the histrion, the juggler; the cabotin can work miracles with his technical mastery; the cabotin keeps alive the tradition of the true art of acting.'[39]

Meyerhold's attempts to revitalise the Russian stage uncannily echo those of nineteenth-century boulevard critics who were admirers of Debureau, and prefigure those of Barrault. One of Meyerhold's most celebrated productions, staged in 1906, was A. Blok's *The Fairground Booth*, in which he used the figures of the *commedia dell'arte* because he saw the 'principles of the fairground booth' as exemplifying the new theatre.[40] The same principles are reflected in *Les Enfants du paradis* which is studded with evocations of the fairground booth, both in the scenes on the Boulevard du Crime and in the use of characters from the *commedia dell'arte*, thereby promoting, as with Meyerhold, anti-naturalistic performance.[41]

Les Enfants du paradis also sets up a strong contrast between movement and talk, or corporeal and verbal expression, which Barrault saw embodied in the contrast between Debureau and Lemaître and which might equally be seen as that between Prévert and Barrault or Carné and Prévert. This contrast is evoked in the conversation between Frédérick and Baptiste shortly after Frédérick has been hired as a replacement lion for the pantomime *Les Dangers de la forêt* at the Funambules. For Frédérick, being forbidden to speak is 'agony when I have an entire orchestra inside me', but he recognises that Baptiste 'speaks with his legs, replies with his hands, with a look, with a shrug'.[42] The nineteenth-century mime theatres were not licensed as 'talkies' for fear that they might compete with other theatrical venues. This silence was so strictly imposed that when the historical Debureau was summoned to court as a result of a duel, huge audiences flocked to hear the celebrated mime's voice for the first time. This restriction is referred to, comically, in the film in the system of fines imposed by the Director of the Funambules. But when Nathalie utters Baptiste's name on stage during the performance of *L'Amoureux de la lune*, she not only transgresses the separation between on and off stage and between pantomime and theatre, she also brings into focus a debate about the future of the cinema which had raged throughout the 1930s.

The advent of sound cinema, strongly condemned by many critics in France especially among Prévert's friends in the Surrealist group, had forced a new approach to performance. The talkies were often felt to be little more than 'filmed theatre' – indeed, they often were little more than film versions of boulevard successes – and the technical restrictions early sound cinema imposed were often felt to limit the expressive resources developed during the silent period. Though *Les Enfants du paradis* is not a conventional narrative film, it nevertheless makes magnificent use of the facility of sound. But it equally celebrates all the lessons of the silent cinema in placing a mime performer at its centre and making him the key sensibility in the film, underlining the cinema's reliance on appearance, gesture and the expressivity of the body.

Jacques Prévert and the Word
The third member of Carné's team was Jacques Prévert, poet, play-wright, painter and occasional actor, who earned his living writing film scripts in the 1930s and 1940s. *Les Enfants du paradis* is one of eight films he wrote for Carné and it is, perhaps, the most typical of his style and sensibility. Prévert's early intellectual and artistic affiliations were with the Surrealist group which he joined in 1925 along with his brother Pierre and his friends Marcel Duhamel and Yves Tanguy. Like many of the group, Prévert was devoted to popular literature and the cinema. He particularly admired serialised thrillers such as Feuillade's *Fantomas* and *Judex* and Jasset's *Nick Carter* and *Zigomar*, and he incorporated writers of popular fiction as characters in *Le Crime de Monsieur Lange* which he wrote for Renoir, and in *Drôle de drame* which he wrote for Carné.

The Feuillade and Jasset films derived from a long tradition of crime literature. Nineteenth-century newspapers made a fortune from '*flics et truands*' (cops and robbers) serialisations such as the memoirs of

François-Eugène Vidocq, simultaneously chief of the Sûreté (the French equivalent of the CID) and master criminal, as well as from fictionalised depictions of low life such as Eugène Sue's blockbuster *Les Mystères de Paris* or Paul Féval's equally successful *Les Mystères de Londres*. One such popular success, the memoirs of Pierre-François Lacenaire published in 1836 under the resounding title *Mémoires, révélations et poésies de Lacenaire, écrits par lui-même à la Conciergerie*, served as one of Prévert's sources for *Les Enfants du paradis*.[43]

In the 1930s Prévert became the mainstay of a left-wing theatre group known as the *Groupe Octobre* for which he wrote the satirical play *La Bataille de Fontenoy* which Carné saw and admired.[44] The play is a denunciation of the rise of fascism in the 1930s, but it appealed to Carné primarily as a radical dramatic experiment: the play incorporates the audience, including its reactions and comments in what is 'performed', and there is a mixture of fictional characters, historical characters and figures from contemporary politics.

Prévert's tastes in popular literature and his dramatic techniques are both reflected in the structure and, to a degree, the content of *Les Enfants du paradis*. The low-life setting of many criminal memoirs and fictions is, of course, reproduced in the '*bar des assassins*' of the Rouge-gorge tavern. But it is in the structure of such serials, based on repetition and recurrence, interspersed with moments of suspense and melodrama, that the real link is to be detected. For like early cops and robbers serials, and indeed like modern-day soap opera, *Les Enfants du paradis* does not progress towards closure but depends on the continual reappearance of the same characters in the same settings in the same or similar situations.[45] Similarly, although the tone of *Les Enfants du paradis* could not be more different from the satirical comedy of *La Bataille de Fontenoy*, the two works have dramaturgical similarities, for, like the play, the film has no difficulty in placing in a dramatic continuum characters modelled on historical originals (Baptiste, Frédérick, Lacenaire) and purely fictional characters such as Garance.

As befits a devotee of pulp fiction, popular speech, proverbs, adages, conventional similes and catch phrases are central to Prévert's film writing and are to be found throughout *Les Enfants du paradis*. His rhetoric is structured around devices of repetition and juxtaposition – anaphora, oxymoron, catachresis and paradox – and one of his preferred techniques is to take a cliché and to repeat or deform it for comic purposes. Such figures are often extended or illuminated by playful visual representations, either taking literally what was a metaphor, or rendering a metaphor comic by demonstrating its incongruity. In this way, alongside the varieties of theatrical production and performance in *Les Enfants du paradis*, we also discover a profusion of textual material woven into an extraordinary verbal collage.

A typical Prevertian conceit is provided early in the film when we first see Arletty incarnating 'Truth' (*la Vérité*). Truth was traditionally represented, as Arletty is here, in the narcissistic pose of a woman looking at herself in a mirror. But the *mise en scène* is also a representation of the proverb that '*la vérité est au fond d'un puits*' (truth is found at the bottom of a well – that is, very hard to find). The fairground barker invites the passers-by to view an abstraction 'come and look at the truth' 'dressed only in herself ' (hence the expression 'the naked truth' in English). This proverb had already been encountered in *Le Jour se lève* where, in the celebrated nude scene, Arletty emerging from her shower is referred to as '*la vérité sortant d'un puits*' (truth coming out of a well). No doubt the more modest depiction of Truth in *Les Enfants du paradis*, and the punters' dissatisfaction with it, are intended as an ironic comment on this episode.

Another, similarly extended and visualised figure of speech, this time of a comic kind, has to do with lions, and is inspired by Frédérick donning the lion skin in the pantomime. First, Frédérick himself says he is a 'specialist in lions' such as 'Richard the Lion Heart, Pygmalion'; next, we catch glimpses, from time to time, of the tavern sign 'Aux Lionceaux du Temple '; finally, the debt-collector attacked by Lacenaire and Avril claims bombastically, if inaccurately, that he defended himself 'like a lion'.

An important visual extension of a verbal commonplace involves the idiom '*violon d'Ingres*' (meaning a hobby or hobby-horse), the work of the painter Ingres who was active at the period the film is set, and (implicitly) Man Ray's painting *Violon d'Ingres* which is itself a visual interpretation of the idiom as it transforms the back of a female nude into a violin. When she is arrested towards the end of Part One, Garance claims that one of her occupations has been artist's [nude] model for 'Monsieur Ingres' who, she says, 'plays the violin in his spare time '. In Part Two, Ingres's orientalism is evoked in the representation of Desdemona who resembles the Thetis in his *Jupiter and Thetis*.

The first exchange between Frédérick and Garance is conducted entirely in cliché. Both parties are good-humouredly conscious of this, which is how we know, and we know they know, that their encounter is not to be taken seriously: 'We've only been together two minutes and you want to leave me already'; 'You're not going to abandon me and leave me all alone'; 'You never know what chance may bring'; 'Paris is so small for those whose love is as great as ours.' This jocular phrase is repeated when Garance and Frédérick meet again by chance, but even such friendly banter, however, has its serious side for it is later revealed to be a privilege that Garance will not accord the Comte de Montray to whom she will not even utter the cliché that she loves him. The various nicknames of the old clothes-seller Jéricho, beginning with 'Jericho' itself – 'Jupiter called Jericho because of the trumpet, called Medusa because of the raft' – make use of the synecdoche common enough where low-life characters are concerned – one thinks of Mack the Knife or Balzac's Trompe-la-mort. But here the figure of speech is not only a mark of Prévert's verbal inventiveness and sheer exuberance, it also illustrates Jericho's protean ability to pop up everywhere, like the fence and informer that Lacenaire, following Baudelaire, alleges he is.[46]

Lacenaire reveals his dramatic talent

In fact, many of the characters, major and minor, live by the word, often specialising in a particular kind of language. The various fairground barkers who stand outside the theatres to lure the public in speak a humorous idolect typified by Anselme Debureau, Baptiste's father, who promises a 'grand, fantastic, exotic, pyrotechnic pantomime'. Jericho, as we have seen, announces his arrival with a series of low-life sobriquets; the authors of *L'Auberge des Adrets* speak in meaninglessly pretentious clichés like Flaubert's Bouvard and Pécuchet; Frédérick parodies theatrical language 'viper memory, knawing regret, red light of forgetfulness', and his love of words can sometimes carry him beyond the bounds of reason and sense. Above all, Lacenaire makes his living through words. In the early part of the film he is a public letter-writer. We hear him composing an epistle for a client who promises he will no longer beat his wife if she will return to him: 'Since you left I am imprisoned in life like a convict in chains' (Lacenaire, of course, served time on the chain gang) – a ridiculous concoction described by the delighted client as 'glorious and moving'. Lacenaire is also a dramatic writer, author of 'a little vaudeville', a genre he prefers to tragedy in which 'people kill one another without causing any harm'. By contrast, Lacenaire causes to flow large quantities of both blood and ink. Like Prévert's Monsieur Lange he embodies the intimate link between crime and writing that found its ultimate expression in melodrama.[47] He is the author-perpetrator of the fiendish crimes which punctuate the narrative of *Les Enfants du paradis*, the first of which is the attack on the debt collector which brings to a close Part One, and the second of which is the murder of the Comte de Montray in the Turkish bath at the end of Part Two. But he is also a man of literature (as was his real-life model). He is not simply the public letter-writer we see in Part One, composing absurdly flowery missives to estranged wives; he is also a dramatic author who, in addition to the 'vaudeville' referred to above, claims, in the conversation in Frédérick's dressing room, to have penned 'a little scene full of laughter and sadness. Two creatures who love each other, lose each other, find each other and lose each other again. A little soft green set, a garden with a fountain ...' From this description we recognise the plot of *L'Amoureux de la lune*, the pantomime in Part One which starred Baptiste, Frédérick and Garance, and, retrospectively, we will recognise the plot of *Les Enfants du paradis* itself which Lacenaire has just rehearsed for Frédérick's benefit. His penchant for melodrama is noted by Frédérick when Avril unexpectedly emerges from behind the screen in the dressing room, for all the world like a character in *L'Auberge des Adrets*, while his talent for dramatic surprise is revealed when he draws back the curtain in the theatre foyer, after Frédérick's triumph as Othello, to show Baptiste and Garance in passionate embrace.

Through Lacenaire, Prévert celebrates an alternative tradition, far removed from the canons of beauty and taste recognised by the Academy or in the official theatre, a tradition whose origins lay in the crime memoirs and popular literature of the 19th century with its cast of criminals and tramps, hangmen and policemen. This is the tradition which enables Frédérick to identify the authors of *L'Auberge des Adrets*, in jocular fashion, as 'the true perpetrators of the crime [of bad writing]', and it is this which positions Lacenaire as the figure of the director/author, the puppet-master pulling strings behind the scenes, in the tale of Harlequin and Columbine which is *Les Enfants du paradis*.

THE THEATRE IN *LES ENFANTS DU PARADIS*

The first and last shots of the film are of a curtain rising and falling and of the camera moving into and pulling back from the stage. The theatre is at the heart of *Les Enfants du paradis*, its structuring principle and its central metaphor. The film itself is a theatrical production which provides the framework or meta-structure within which a succession of theatrical performances in different genres – mime, pantomime, melodrama, tragedy – are offered to our gaze and are superimposed and interwoven to form a narrative. In Part One we see parts of *Les Dangers de la forêt* (the dangers of the forest) in which Baptiste takes over as Pierrot and Frédérick is hired to replace the lion who has walked out, and *L'Amoureux de la lune* (the lover of the moon) starring Baptiste as Pierrot, Frédérick as Harlequin, Garance as Phoebe/Artemis/Columbine, and Nathalie as the laundress. In Part Two Frédérick stars in the melodrama *L'Auberge des Adrets* and in Shakespeare's *Othello*, while Baptiste stars in the pantomime *Chand d'habits* (old clothes-seller). In addition to these productions we are also shown two spontaneous performances, Baptiste's re-enactment of the theft of the watch on the Boulevard, which saves Garance from arrest, and Lacenaire's revelation of Baptiste and Garance embracing outside the theatre in which

Frédérick has starred as Othello. The performers and the genres reflect those central to the theatre of the July Monarchy – Frédérick, for example, opened in *L'Auberge des Adrets* at the Ambigu-Comique on 2 July 1823 – but though they all took place, they did not necessarily follow the chronological order of the film, and this suggests that their presentation has a thematic rather than a historical interest.

An understanding of the social and political role of the theatre under the July Monarchy throws some light on this question. By the 1830s the theatre had become the major form of public entertainment in Paris. A revolutionary decree of 1791 had enabled anyone to open a theatre, while the abolition of censorship in 1830 made the theatre even more popular. However, there were essentially two kinds of theatre in Paris and their rivalry, referred to from time to time in the film, provides the explanation for some of the events depicted. There was, on the one hand, the state-subsidised sector consisting of the Opéra, the Théâtre-Français (Comédie Française) and the Théâtre de l'Odéon, and, on the other, the so-called 'Boulevard'. The distinction between these two sectors was historical, geographical and financial; it was reflected in different repertoires and, to some extent, different audiences. The

4 2   Frédérick (right) as Robert Macaire

subsidised sector pre-dated the Revolution, it was situated away from the boulevards (in the case of the Odéon, very disadvantageously on the Left Bank), and its repertoire was essentially classical and neoclassical, consisting of Molière, Racine, some Marivaux, a little Corneille, Voltaire's tragedies and contemporary neoclassical tragedy. By contrast, what might be called the private sector specialised in vaudeville (a combination of pantomime and operetta), melodrama and, later, Romantic theatre. Its centres were the Théâtre de la Gaîté, where many of Pixérécourt's melodramas were performed, the Théâtre de l'Ambigu-Comique, where Frédérick starred in *L'Auberge des Adrets*, the Théâtre des Funambules (tightrope walkers), which, as its name suggests, specialised in circus acts and mime and where Debureau was the star attraction, and the Théâtre de la Porte-Saint-Martin, which began life as a centre for melodrama but gradually specialised in Romantic drama. The first three of these theatres were sited on the Boulevard du Temple and the last was close by.[48]

By the 1830s the subsidised sector had been deserted by virtually all of its audience; it was artistically as well as financially bankrupt, and had lost whatever central cultural function it had had before the Revolution.[49] But on the Boulevard, Romantic theatre and melodrama attracted an audience drawn from a cross-section of the population, from the 'people' as well as the bourgeoisie and the aristocracy, and its mixture of text and song, which gradually became conventionalised in the Restoration period, turned it into a moralistic and stylised kind of popular tragedy.[50] The search for a form of entertainment that would not only be popular but nationally significant is one of the underlying concerns of Carné and his collaborators, and in their *mise en scène* of the evolution of the nineteenth-century stage they sought to draw parallels between the theatre and the cinema which was its successor.

One of the means by which *Les Enfants du paradis* links nineteenth-century theatre history to the contemporary period is through the melodramatic tradition. Melodrama is seen in the film in the shape of *L'Auberge des Adrets*. This wooden play by Benjamin Antier, whose authors in the film are parodied like Flaubert's Bouvard and Pécuchet, was turned into a tremendous hit when Frédérick played the role of the bandit Robert Macaire for laughs. Frédérick's dishevelled attire in the role of Macaire, attributed in the film to a brawl with his creditors just before appearing on stage, became the actor's trademark.

The successive revivals of *Robert Macaire*, by popular demand, underline how closely nineteenth-century theatre resembled twentieth-century cinema in its creation of stars and its exploitation of hot literary properties. At the same time, the fact that Macaire is a bandit and an outlaw, an emblematic man of the people who mocks literary and political authority, both an actor in the drama and a mordant critic of it, points equally to the transgressive potential of the melodramatic genre in the 19th century and its subversive potential in the twentieth-century cinema.

The film's references to the Romantic theatre are just as ideologically significant. Authors such as Victor Hugo wished to revolutionise the theatre because it was simultaneously the most noble and the most widely accessible genre of the age, the literary form in which political and cultural debates were conducted. In the hands of Victor Hugo and his contemporaries, Romantic theatre accomplished a thematic, formal and intellectual revolution. Its privileged terrain was History – the representation of key moments in the history of the French nation, and sometimes of other nations, with the ambition, as in Hugo's *Cromwell*, of offering a total picture of an era, the 'total resurrection of the past' dreamed of by the historian Michelet. Romantic theatre had two new preoccupations: the fact, made evident through the Revolution, that the People had become the actors of History; and the nature of heroism, embodied most often in a great man (Napoleon, Cromwell, Hernani, the actor Kean) whose subjective experience is the mainspring of the drama. This is why Frédérick, in his ambition to become a great actor, dreams of roles such as Charles the Bold, Attila, Henry IV and Ravaillac.

The English theatre was an important influence in the pursuit of these ambitions. Letourneur's new translation of Shakespeare began to appear in France in 1777, prefaced by the influential critic Guizot's *Eloge de Shakespeare*. An English theatre company visited in Paris in July 1822, performing *Othello* (among other plays) at the Porte-Saint-Martin. The physical expressiveness of English acting styles was considered vulgar, while Shakespeare's failure to observe the dramatic unities, and his recourse to popular rather than elevated language, created a public scandal (reference to Desdemona's 'handkerchief' was particularly derided). But although the English approach to the theatre was so different from that officially recognised by the Théâtre-Français, it showed the Romantics how the French theatre might be revived. By

1828, when the English players returned, their season was a triumph, so much so that the poet Alfred de Vigny's 'Lettre à Lord X' held *Othello* up as an example of what the new theatre should be, and in 1829 the Comédie Française performed his translation of it, *Le More de Venise*, to considerable acclaim.

These historical events help us to understand better the fictional Frédérick's obsession with producing *Othello* and playing the leading role in it. Throughout the film, in passing references to Garance as 'my Desdemona', or to the similarity between the name 'Baptiste' and the 'batiste handkerchief', the play becomes a touchstone not just for Frédérick's understanding of the relationship between Garance and Baptiste but for the emotional inspiration of his own art and that of the new theatre. For it is the combination of the popular and the elevated, and the experience of extreme or excessive emotion, which finds its ultimate expression in the scene where Othello murders his wife, that is both the defining characteristic of melodrama and what enables Frédérick to act as a new kind of hero.

THE PERFORMER AS HERO: FRÉDÉRICK AND DEBUREAU

If the dandy Lacenaire was the living embodiment of the connexion between art and crime, a disciple of De Quincey and, in Théophile Gautier's words, a 'gutter Manfred', Frédérick and Debureau were performers in whose careers the ideological thrust of popular drama was achieved, and it is therefore hardly surprising that they should play a central role in the film. They are *'enfants' 'du paradis'* – children of the 'gods' in the theatre, or the popular audience – in terms of their personal origins, the popular appeal of their performances, and their role as projections of the popular imagination. Both were instrumental in revolutionising performance in the nineteenth-century theatre to create a kind of popular heroism, and both became legends in their own time.

The historical Frédéric Lemaître was the son of an architect, born in 1800 in Le Havre. He began acting at the age of fifteen and attempted to join the Odéon company when he was nineteen. Having failed to do so he worked, briefly, as the lion in the pantomime *Pyramus et Thisbe* (hence the jocular references to lions in the film). Subsequently, Frédérick anglicised his name, perhaps in admiration for English theatre, and although did not have much success with state companies, he pursued a glorious career, principally at the Porte Saint-Martin where he ends up in the film, playing many of the leading roles in Romantic drama as well as in celebrated melodramas.

Frédérick became central to Hugo's attack on the traditional theatre much of which took place through set-piece 'battles' at the performances of *Cromwell* (1827) and *Hernani* (1830) and the accompanying literature of justification (*Préface de Cromwell*, 1827). Critics often complained that the actors at the Théâtre-Français were too old and that they would not or could not adapt their performing style to new theatrical requirements. This meant that during the 1830s new writing tended to be performed on the Boulevard. Hugo became a great admirer of Frédérick and conceived the central roles in many of his plays with the actor in mind, casting him as Gennaro in *Lucrèce Borgia* (1832) which was Frédérick's greatest triumph. For Hugo, the actor embodied the physical and mental contrasts, the simultaneously aristocratic and popular appeal, that was the foundation of Romantic theatre as the poet conceived it. His range was infinitely greater than that permitted by the Théâtre-Français and he was capable of playing in all registers, appealing to all audiences.

Debureau's fame was also based on his capacity to extend the range of theatre and to appeal to a broad cross-section of the public. Just as Romantic theatre aimed to be a truly popular art, so mime appeared to extend its significance outwards. According to Debureau's most recent biographer, the mime artist was born in Amiens in 1796 and was the son of a family of circus artists whose speciality, as was that of most circus owners until 1850 or thereabouts, was performing on the tightrope,[51] and it was only because he was unable to walk the tightrope that the son became a mime. To do this he simplified the traditional Pierrot look by dispensing with the frilly collar and baggy pants, and at the same time heightened the visual contrasts by replacing the traditional white wool bonnet with a black skullcap that emphasised the startling whiteness of his face, modulating the appearance of the mime from the comic to the tragic and rendering it more emotionally expressive.

One of the sources for the character of Baptiste in *Les Enfants du paradis*, was an essay written by the nineteenth-century theatre critic

Jules Janin, *Debureau, histoire du théâtre à quatre sous*,[52] which made the mime and his performances famous with the literary community of the July Monarchy. For Janin, the true theatre was to be found on the Boulevard in the badly lit, badly equipped halls frequented by poor people who shouted and screamed at the actors and contributed noisily to the play, and not in the well-behaved, plushly furnished, but moribund corridors of the Théâtre-Français. For Janin, Debureau 'is the people's actor and the people's friend, revolutionary like the people with his self-possession and his dumb sarcasm which lend him his immense superiority'; 'Gilles is the people and it is the people that Debureau represents in all his plays.'

With such fulsome praise it mattered little that Janin had, if George Sand is to be believed, invented most of Debureau's history,[53] for a fashion was born. Gautier went further in his essay 'Shakespeare aux Funambules', published in 1842, in which he compares the pantomime *Chand d'habits*, which is performed in the film, to *Hamlet* and *Macbeth*.[54] 'As Pierrot walks down the road in his white tunic, his white pants, and with his powdered face, preoccupied with vague desires, he is surely the symbol of the unsullied and still innocent human soul, tormented by its aspiration towards higher realms.'[55] Concurring with Janin that here was to be found the real vitality of the theatre, he nevertheless emphasised more than his fellow critic had done the collective nature of the spectacle: 'Everyone is the author of these marvellous shows; this is the author, prompter and above all the audience, a collective being who has more wit than Voltaire, Beaumarchais or Byron.'[56] Baptiste in the film is potentially all these things: he is the butt of his father's sarcasm, he has a sense of social justice and family responsibility, but he is also a tormented soul, prey to self-hatred, unable to resist the powerful appeal of the woman whom he had found and then lost, and whom he miraculously finds again.

THEATRE AS MEMORY AND REPETITION

In *Les Enfants du paradis* the theatre is used to pose the central questions of truth and identity, through repetition, re-enactment and memory. At the beginning and at the end of the film we enter and leave the diegetic space on the Boulevard du Temple and there is an obvious tension between our knowledge of its artificiality and the brilliance of the reconstruction. How seriously are we to take the events enacted within this set? What kind of realism is offered to our view within this theatre? The question of veracity is posed at the outset. 'Truth' is already posited as relative and contingent, *one* of the many attractions available in a booth on the Boulevard. This is when we encounter Arletty sitting three-quarters submerged in a barrel of water with her naked shoulders exposed to view. The appeal of this attraction waned, as we later discover; audiences were disappointed because this was not the whole or the 'naked' Truth but only Truth 'shoulder deep' (not reaching the heart, perhaps). And so Truth emerges from her barrel and mingles with the crowd where she becomes 'Garance' whose various encounters, throughout the length of the film, provide the narrative thread. It is as though, dissatisfied with partial revelation, Truth has gone in search of more artistically and poetically satisfying narratives – different truths and compromised truths – which are exposed to our view.

Just as the set is deliberately utopian so are many of the characters in it. With the exception of that of Garance, their identities are, to be sure, based on historical characters. But the film does not present these characters as the subject of biography or seek to explain their actions by recourse to psychology. It offers, instead, historical 'figures' around whom there have accreted generations of myth and tradition. The characters in *Les Enfants du paradis* are like the '*images d'Epinal*' which illustrated popular picture books in the 19th century, and like those found in forms of popular entertainment such as historical tableaux or waxworks museums. In fact, they are like the figures of the early cinema that offered re-enactments, in tableaux form, of the high points of history and famous historical figures, such as the murder of the Duc de Guise or the death of Marie-Antoinette. Agitprop theatre as Brecht devised it, or Prévert understood it in *La Bataille de Fontenoy*, is inspired by the same popular modes, although it uses them for political purposes.

In such forms of art, narrative takes the form of repetition, and psychological interpretation is an irrelevance. The reader or viewer does not challenge, and would not wish to challenge, the verisimilitude of the work of art, and is not shocked by inaccuracies or anachronisms. Instead, what is important is that the figures and situations should be entirely as expected, that the truth of the portrait should derive from its conformity to an existing model, and that narrative closure should be continually postponed. The characterisation, plot and narrative structure of *Les Enfants du paradis* are based on these techniques of popular exemplarity. Where the film differs from earlier models, especially cinematic ones (but where arguably it prefigures later versions such as soap opera), is that its protagonists are not kings, queens and politicians, but actors from the stage, and that the history enacted is that of performances not politics.

But the appeal to the heightened realism of memory is not confined to the viewers of the film; it is also made by and to the actors within it. It is an important effect of the division of the film into two parts. For the second part takes place, we are told, after 'several years' have gone by. This means that the various actors are placed in a position of remembering what went before. In retrospect therefore, as we watch the second part, the entire first part becomes a projection of memory: 'In years gone by' says Lacenaire, 'A whole period'; and Garance agrees nostalgically: 'Easy years, happy days, the sweetness of life',[57] the last phrase, of course, conventionally evoking a time 'before the Revolution'. And in conversation with Frédérick, Garance associates memory with the city: 'I love only Paris. Paris and its memories.'[58]

The actors' greater maturity is signified in subtle physical transformations which emphasise the passage of time but are often revealed to be costume effects, disguises of a more or less convincing kind. To play the part of Othello, Frédérick acquires a beard and pads his torso; to play the lovesick clown Baptiste is dressed in the smart jacket and breeches he has stolen from the old clothes-seller, and while waiting in the wings, attired in this costume, talks to Frédérick of his wife, his child and his professional success. As for Garance, she who has travelled furthest to Scotland and to India, her appearance has changed from that of a young girl in a checked frock to that of a mature, sophisticated, and expensively dressed woman, yet she too appears incognito, veiled and unrecognised by those around her, a mysterious *femme du monde*.

Garance's conversations with Frédérick, with Lacenaire and finally, when they do meet, with Baptiste, are suffused with nostalgia. In Madame Hermine's lodging house it is important that Garance and Baptiste take the same room where 'everything is the same, nothing has changed'. There they live their first and only night of love as a re-enactment of their earlier encounter. This is clearly the world of dreams and the unconscious: when Baptiste and Garance first walked on the Barrière de Ménilmontant their meeting was 'like a dream' for Baptiste when Garance

5 0   Frédérick as Harlequin; Garance as Moon Goddess

recalled her childhood and her past, and when, in her room at Madame Hermine's, he told her he dreamed of 'impossible' things. Now the structure of their second encounter echoes that of the first with the same reference to the 'little gleam' that Garance saw in the twinkling lights of Ménilmontant and that Baptiste now detects in her eyes. And in Baptiste all that is repressed, his love for Garance, his desire, is reactivated and returns in physical form.

Memories, repressed desires, and recollections 'embellished by memory' as Nathalie says of Garance, largely determine what happens in Part Two of the film, forcing a rereading of Part One as a projection back into the past of a realisation of desire. If the second half of the film is a replay or a re-enactment of the first, the first is a *répétition* – in the French sense of a rehearsal – of the second. The outcome is equally unsatisfactory in both cases. This is a recurrent dream in which the passage of time is an irrelevance and in which certain motifs, desires, and repressed elements recur in similar or in different configurations. Thus the theatrical tropes and performances are used to underline the way in which the film – and by extension cinema – is the theatre of the unconscious, so that the performances of the first part are echoed in those of the second, and events off stage (in the waking world) are uncannily mirrored or uncannily prefigure those on stage/in the cinema (in the dream world).

If we consider the distribution of the performances, we can see that the pantomimes of the first half, *Les Dangers de la forêt* and *L'Amoureux de la lune* are variations on the *commedia dell'arte* theme. The first demonstrates in comic fashion how life on stage and off stage can become hopelessly entwined. After one of the mimes hits another too hard on stage, a brawl ensues which results in the Barrigni family deserting the Funambules for their great rivals the Saqui troupe across the road, thereby giving chances both to Frédérick who takes over the part of the Lion/Harlequin and to Baptiste who hitherto has not been allowed by his father to appear on stage but now becomes Pierrot. By the time of *L'Amoureux de la lune*, Frédérick, Garance and Baptiste are all in place as Harlequin, Columbine and Pierrot, in which guise they re-enact the events that took place the night before at Madame Hermine's lodging house. There Baptiste metaphorically places Garance on the pedestal and fails to make love to her; while in the pantomine she literally stands on one. While he sleeps, Harlequin comes along and talks her down just as Frédérick had persuaded her not to spend the night alone but with him. Seeing she has departed he feels suicidal and tries to hang himself. But he is saved by Nathalie (who, as the brightly domestic laundress, has other uses for the macabre rope), just as in Part Two she will save Baptiste from suicide using Madame Hermine as intermediary. Indeed, it is Nathalie who underscores the way in which Frédérick, Baptiste and Garance in the film are fulfilling the pantomime plot for, when she realises that Baptiste is looking into the wings where Frédérick is deep in amorous conversation with Garance, she breaks all the rules and utters Baptiste's name on stage, bringing about the confusion of genres which the system of theatrical codes and privileges had attempted to conserve but which reality undermined on all sides.

Like *L'Amoureux de la lune*, *Chand d'habits* is a *mise en abyme* of *Les Enfants du paradis* which mirrors and magnifies the structure and *mise en scène* of the pantomime. In the original version, commented on by Gautier, Pierrot killed the old clothes-seller who returned to haunt him in macabre fashion, his ghost appearing in the prompter's box in the middle of his performance. In *Chand d'habits*, as Baptiste performs it here, the old clothes-seller is well and truly killed, but the living Jéricho, like some ghastly superego, returns to haunt Baptiste as he tries to run after Garance through the carnival crowd at the end of the film, urging him to remember his family responsibilities and his career. Similarly, in *Othello* the Moor smothers Desdemona in her bed and the curtain falls to tumultuous applause for Frédérick's virtuoso performance. But then Lacenaire draws back the curtain of the theatre foyer to reveal outside, on the other stage, in the 'other scene' of Freudian dreams, the infidelity of Garance, the 'other' Desdemona, with Baptiste. Which of these performances is theatre and which life, which is inside and which outside, which is the present and which is recollection infused with desire?

GENDER AND GENRE: THE POLITICS OF IDENTITY
. . . .

The series of theatrical performances, loosely connected by history, are brought into close relation by Garance whose peregrinations and adventures, whose passage from man to man in acts of love or prostitution, and whose chance encounters – with Baptiste, Frédérick, Lacenaire, Montray – lend the film a skeleton structure. She is, first and

Garance as jeune ingénue

Garance as Indian Queen

Garance as Marlene Dietrich

Garance lets her hair down

foremost, a narrative figure, enabling the male characters to become what they are or are destined to be. Emerging from her tent on the Boulevard, this embodiment of the partial truth captivates, in turn, all the men she meets: Frédérick is won over by her smile, Baptiste because she throws him a rose, the Comte de Montray by her appearance in *L'Amoureux de la lune*. Lacenaire, meanwhile, calls her his guardian angel and seeks her as his demonic muse. Her function is to elicit their performances and to institute the work of imagination and fantasy on which they depend, so that her presence helps Baptiste reveal his gift for mime, it inspires Frédérick to play Othello, it allows Lacenaire to reveal his talent for drama and *mise en scène*. She is the source of the different performance genres through which the film progresses, but throughout her vicissitudes she remains an enigmatic character and though all say they love her it is hard to know what or whom they love.

With the exception of Arletty, the performers in the film enact what they are in more ways than one. As characters they have allotted roles which they learn to perform with greater or lesser degrees of success, roles which we judge by their conformity and exemplarity. But the cast list was chosen for its conformity to off-screen type as well, and some of the real-life habits and tastes of the performers are knowingly, if obliquely, referred to in the film narrative: thus Pierre Brasseur (Frédérick) was known for his drinking and Jean-Louis Barrault (Baptiste) for his physical exercises; Marcel Herrand (Lacenaire) was a homosexual like the master criminal whose part he acted, while Maria Casarès (Nathalie) was hopelessly in love with Herrand who was not attracted by her. Arletty had a Nazi lover, who may or may not have inspired the Comte de Montray, while Robert Le Vigan, the original choice for Jéricho, was a notorious collaborator. The coincidences are such that the interpenetration of life and art becomes one of the film's major themes.

Arletty, on the other hand, is cast against type. Before the war, she had a reputation for comedy. She had twice played a warm-hearted prostitute for Carné as Madame Raymonde in *Hôtel du nord* and as Clara in *Le Jour se lève*, with both roles, but especially that of Madame Raymonde, capitalising on her pre-war reputation as one of the most celebrated exponents of Parisian *gouaille*, or street humour, an *enfant de Paris* in her own right. A change of register came with Carné's first wartime film *Les Visiteurs du soir* in which he exploited the apparent contradiction between her physical appearance and her raucous voice as a gender ambiguity by disguising her as a (mature) woman dressed as a (page) boy. *Les Enfants du paradis* trades on the uncertainty and ambiguity surrounding both the actress Arletty and the character Garance. It exploits the assumption that an audience will be familiar with her ambiguous gender in *Les Visiteurs du soir* and her *demi-mondaine* role in *Hôtel du nord* and *Le Jour se lève*, just as it is familiar with the on and off-screen roles of many of the other actors. In this way, it juxtaposes a group of male actors who are cast 'true to type' with a female star who is not. Garance's cool irony contrasts with Arletty's wit and repartee in the earlier films, the distant *femme du monde* with the earlier tarts with hearts of gold. And though she is beautiful she is emphatically not a *jeune première* (Arletty was aged 44 when shooting began); she has an agelessness which is modified by her various costumes in the film, and which is a crucial component of her enigmatic quality.

Unlike the other characters we have no model for Garance. We know her pedigree but we are ignorant of what she has or will become. We know she was happy in her idyllic youth in Ménilmontant, but we also know that she grew up fast in the big city to become a creature of expediency, accepting Baptiste's offer to find her a room in Madame Hermine's house, Frédérick's company for the night, a role in *L'Amoureux de la lune*, and the protection of the Comte de Montray. She thus embodies the tension between innocence and experience, ignorance and knowledge, that is set out in the film.

Garance's uncertain or unknowable identity, her capacity to play the parts others give her, foregrounds the central theme of the film. Virtually all the characters are masters of disguise, swopping roles at will, making their living by pretending to be someone else, or, like Montray, playing a social role to the hilt. In some cases the assumption of identity is comically over-determined, as when Frédérick gets inside the lion's skin; in others, like Jéricho's, it is a matter of hearsay, rumour, reputation, or indeed, self-designation. Identity is generally a matter of memory and appearance; merely a theatrical property. Thus Lacenaire, the supreme master of self-reinvention, cannot keep track of his aliases and is startled when Garance addresses him as 'Pierre-François'. 'I've so many names,' he says, 'that I sometimes can't remember them myself'. Jéricho, on the other hand, is incensed that Anselme Debureau has

'stolen his identity', even though he himself supplied the 'clothes' for it.
'I didn't know what use you would make of it,' protests Jéricho.[59] But
Garance is not a person who reinvents herself: she is a fiction or
projection of other people's invention, so that when summoned by the
police to say who she is she replies 'They call me Garance'. It is an alias
that others have invented.

Garance has the capacity to incarnate the projections of other
imaginations. At times, she recalls the *grisette* Mimi Pinson in the short
story by Musset or the Mimi of Murger's *Scènes de la vie de Bohème*,[60] but
her various guises derive mainly from the iconography of the cinema
and her radical transformations point to the different avatars of 'woman'
on screen. We see her as the *jeune ingénue* in a gingham dress with
smocked bodice and puffed sleeves, like the worthy fiancée of the silent
cinema; we see her as an immobile nude contemplating her own beauty;
as the statuesque moon goddess Artemis on her pedestal. When she
wraps Madame Hermine's bedspread around her in sari fashion, she is an
Indian queen – a prospective reference to the voyages she is later said to
have made to India with the Comte de Montray, and another element in
the orientalism also evoked in *Othello* or the Turkish baths. When she

sits, veiled, in the theatre box, night after night to watch Baptiste perform, she is filmed as Sternberg filmed Marlene Dietrich in *The Devil is Woman* (1935). When she leaves the boulevard in her carriage, having abandoned Baptiste, she resembles Merle Oberon as Anne Boleyn in Korda's *The Private Lives of Henry VIII* (1933). As the mysterious, unknown woman she has affinities with the women in film noir, and she is the *femme fatale* whose kiss is capable of causing death. Each of these is a partial truth, 'shoulder deep' as the fairground barker put it; each presents Garance as increasingly cold, distant, narcissistic and self-sufficient, exploiting the impression first created by the self-contained circular movement of the barrel in which she sits as Truth, emphasised by her hieratic untouchability on the pedestal in *L'Amoureux de la lune*. Many of these images also film her slightly from below and appear increasingly two-dimensional, framing her face as though in a picture without perspective, placing her flatly against the back of the carriage, or the box of the theatre, the set of the pantomime, or the circus tent, so as to emphasise her iconic status. She is, as Anne Freadman put it, 'a sign of herself designating her own absence in the framed and separate image of art'.[61]

Perhaps, however, we can best understand Garance from what must surely be the major intertextual reference of the film, Victor Fleming's *Gone with the Wind* (1939). As is recalled in Jean-Pierre Melville's *L'Armée des ombres*, in occupied France *Gone with the Wind* acquired a mythic status analogous to that of *Citizen Kane*.[62] There are many points of comparison between Carné's and Fleming's films. Both are set at a time of civil war, a defining moment of national history, and both represent the most ambitious and spectacular productions of their generation. There are many resemblances of detail, too. The highly unusual name 'Garance', which is glossed for us in *Les Enfants du paradis* as 'the name of a flower', a flower which is 'as red as your lips', is, in fact, the colour of the scarlet used for soldiers' trousers in the 19th century. By the same token, Garance is surely a French Scarlett O'Hara, a woman similarly buffeted by war, torn between two men, one who is swashbuckling and the other sensitive, obliged to prostitute herself to survive.[63]

The comparison with *Gone with the Wind* can help to understand *Les Enfants du paradis* as a melodrama in which the star-crossed lovers lose each other at the end in a scene guaranteed to bring tears to the eyes.

But as we attempt to read it as a melodrama, we inevitably notice significant variations from the genre developed by Selznick in Hollywood, so much so that it can be understood as an ironic interrogation of the Hollywood conventions. Unlike most melodramas, at least of the Hollywood variety, *Les Enfants du paradis* is not a 'woman's film' of the kind Selznick specialised in. The female viewer, to whom such movies were primarily addressed, invests in Scarlett, just as she desires the satanic lover incarnated by Clark Gable. But the key sensibility in *Les Enfants du paradis* belongs not to Garance but Baptiste. It is not Garance we feel for, as she departs in her carriage at the end, but Baptiste, the sad clown, whose brief night of passion is destined to be his last. In other words, in *Les Enfants du paradis* the dispositions of the melodramatic imagination, as we have been led to expect them in the Hollywood cinema, are turned on their head.

What this means can be understood if we recall how closely the thematics of the mirror are associated with Garance. The mirror emphasises her solipsism and explains why, as a character, she is strangely lifeless, a montage of iconic images, memories of women culled from the repertoire of American and European cinema. She is depicted, from the outset, as a distant and self-absorbed 'moon goddess' and she becomes progressively colder as the film advances, refusing to say the words 'I love you' to the Comte de Montray. Indeed, the only time she lets her hair down – literally – is when she tells Montray her heart belongs to Baptiste. But this message is visually challenged, even as she confides it, since it is accompanied by an image which shows her contemplating her own face in the mirror.

The mirror, however, is also a figure of inversion – the truth will be the inverted image of what is seen in the mirror. Understanding Garance as an inverted image – or an image of inversion – helps to illuminate much that is obscure or unconvincing about her role in *Les Enfants du paradis*. For though this is a melodrama, it inverts the central proposition on which Hollywood melodrama is based, that 'woman' is the site of pathos, the vessel of excessive emotion, or the embodiment of a dysfunctional society. Carné gives a different twist to this plot because he places a man at its centre. Uniquely, perhaps, in the history of the cinema, *Les Enfants du paradis* is a melodrama about men, a melodrama whose structural dispositions are inverted in relation to representations of gender.

Baptiste in *Chand d'Habits*

Jéricho: spectre at the feast

Thus in this film Baptiste is placed in the female role, as is indicated in his first bedraggled appearance when, as the masochistic butt of paternal abuse, he sits disguised in a long wig and tail coat, while Garance is positioned in the male role.[64] Both, in fact, try different gender roles as appropriate: Nathalie, seeing Baptiste has been smitten by love, asks 'Is it a woman?', to which Baptiste replies 'I don't know'.[65] When Frédérick tells Garance he preferred her first costume she replies, 'All tastes are natural.'[66] When Baptiste adopts a stance of aggressive masculinity, waiting in the wings to perform *Chand d'habits*, he is accused by Jéricho of stealing his appearance, but after learning that Garance has returned he collapses into sartorial disarray. Each of them tries on womanliness or manliness, adopting it as a masquerade.[67] But as befits a mirror image, the various repetitions and rehearsals throughout the film stand in inverted relation to one another. Lacenaire links the image of inversion to memories resurfacing in a way that can be disturbing or cruel when he warns Garance: ' Be careful, my angel, it is not a good idea to look backwards. You turn back to your past and it jumps in your face like an angry cat.'[68] Nowhere is this clearer than in the final scene of the film which is a back-to-front action replay – or a projection – of the first nocturnal encounter between Garance and Baptiste in Madame Hermine's lodging house. In Part One Baptiste shielded his eyes and, like Orpheus, turned his back to avoid gazing on his lover; in Part Two, it is Garance who turns her back and Baptiste who, like Eurydice, is swallowed up into the Paradise/underworld of the Boulevard.

Critics of *Les Enfants du paradis* generally confine themselves to elucidating a 'homosexual subtext' in the film by pointing, for example, to homoerotic encounters such as the one between Frédérick and Lacenaire in Frédérick's dressing-room or to the fact that the character of Lacenaire was inspired by a historical figure who was implicated in the notorious murder of a male prostitute in a Turkish bath.[69] In this, the film resembles others by Carné and Prévert who both enjoyed the verbal and visual jokes associated with sexual ambiguity.

However, the ambiguity of gender roles is much more thorough-going in *Les Enfants du paradis* than in any previous Carné film except *Les Visiteurs du soir* and much more subtle than in that earlier example. Considering gender as performance in *Les Enfants du paradis* not only permits a much more playful reading of the film but a much more convincing one, providing a better understanding of Garance and rendering her relationship to Baptiste and the reactions of Baptiste and Nathalie much more persuasive. For as a psychological character, or even as a fatally beautiful woman, Garance hardly comes alive, but as a figure of inversion, a projection of Baptiste's homosexual desire (and, on occasion, that of others) she is entirely convincing.

The perception that in erotic triangles, the psychologically and sexually intense relationships may, despite folk wisdom, just as easily be homosocial or homosexual as heterosexual, and be based on 'gender asymmetry', so that there may be uncertainty about the member of the triangle who is the real object of desire, helps to elucidate events in the film.[70] Viewed in this light, Baptiste's Orphic horror at the thought of seeing Garance undress, Nathalie's conviction that she will marry Baptiste though he does not love her and, after the interlude in which Baptiste does indeed become the father of a family, her despair at his 'reversion' to Garance, all become much more poignant if Baptiste is seen not as wrestling with a decision to leave his wife but struggling with the nature of his desire.

Indeed, the triangle as 'a useful figure by which the "common-sense" of our intellectual tradition schematizes erotic relations'[71] is extensively worked through in the permutations which arise as the characters in *Les Enfants du paradis* try on and play with gender roles. [72] The object of desire – or the 'point' of the triangle in the spatial metaphor – is usually Garance and sometimes Lacenaire, the two characters whose fundamental solitude, and fundamental similarity is consistently emphasised. But in repressed form it is also Jéricho, the 'third party', the spectre at the feast, the man whom no-one wants (he laments the fact that he cannot find a wife), the link in the chain that many would prefer to break, fortune-teller, palm-reader and interpreter of dreams.

THE VIEWER FROM *FLÂNEUR* TO VOYEUR
. . . .

In addition to offering a commonsense representation of erotic relations, however, the triangle is also a spatial representation of socio-political configurations and a means of cultural interpretation, a means of relating a visual regime to an economy of desire.

Lacenaire leaves Garance as Montray arrives

All the plays and pantomimes performed in the film incorporate the figure of the viewer. The repeated shots of theatre boxes, inhabited by different spectators according to the performance witnessed, emphasise the degree to which the audience's perception is an essential component of interpretation. We, as the audience of the film, are not allowed to forget that these are plays within plays, and that, even if the styles of acting and set design were not there to recall the fact, these are performances. The frequent positioning of the camera at the back of the theatre, cutting between performers and, often rowdy, audiences, as well as the point of view which embraces within the frame the privileged audience in their boxes and the performers on stage, are all there to recall the profound imbrication of one within the other. At various moments in the first half of the film, real life erupts into performances, as in the brawl between the Saqui and the Barrigni during *Les Dangers de la forêt*, or when Baptiste and Nathalie see Garance conversing with Frédérick in the wings of the Funambules. In the second part of the film performance enters real life as when Frédérick, in the role of Macaire, turns into a critical commentator on the play in which he is performing, or when Baptiste collapses on stage on learning that Garance has returned. The on-stage, off-stage link is particularly evident in the complex series of visual parallels established in the relationship between Garance and the two dandies Montray and Lacenaire. Thus Lacenaire pays a visit to Garance, ascending the majestic flight of steps in her house which resembles the flight of steps we later see Frédérick descend in the theatre foyer. Montray quizzes Garance as to whether this mysterious visitor is the object of her love while she is sitting at a dressing table that is placed in an alcove draped with curtains like the proscenium arch of a theatre. Othello murders Desdemona who is reclining on a four-poster bed draped with curtains that resemble the fairground booths we have seen on the Boulevard, whereupon Montray, whose bearded profile has been compared to Othello's in a rapid cut from one to the other, goes down the stairs into the theatre foyer whose curtains are drawn back to reveal Garance's infidelity with Baptiste.

These *mises en scène* obey the principle of inversion encountered elsewhere. When an actor comes off stage and joins the ranks of the authors/spectators he does so from an opposite, or inverted point of view. So that whereas Montray when watching Garance, Garance when watching Baptiste, and Montray and Garance when watching Frédérick all do so from the box on the left-hand side of the theatre, Macaire takes over the box on the right-hand side of the theatre in order to deliver his critical comments on *L'Auberge des Adrets*, while the prefiguration of Garance's betrayal is not only presented as a performance within the spontaneously theatrical space of an alcove but the performance we see, as her reflection suggests, is a mirror image.

Les Enfants du paradis charts the process of inversion by which the viewer changed from the nineteenth-century *flâneur* into the voyeur, from the active seeker after unexpected knowledge and connoisseur of urban modernity, into an illicit spectator of hidden acts. The opening scenes of the film and the characters in them are deliberately reminiscent of Baudelaire's prose poems 'Les Foules'[73] and 'Le Vieux Saltim-banque'[74] which celebrate the *flâneur*, while Baptiste is first shown as a Baudelairian hero, since his thirst for social and sexual knowledge when he enters the peepshow to inspect Garance is typical of the exercise of 'power [by] the seeing, bourgeois male'.[75] Baptiste continues in the role of viewer when he witnesses Lacenaire picking a watch from the pocket of an unsus-pecting passer-by, and at the *barrière* where he tells the 'blind' beggar Fil de soie that the purpose of his nocturnal wanderings is

'to see'. But in the Rouge-gorge, Baptiste's spectatorial role is denied. Jéricho tells him 'you don't belong here', and Avril forcibly ejects him from the tavern. He leaves with Garance who assumes the role of *flâneur* in his place. This is another indication of gender inversion since she takes on what is always the male role in the literature of urbanity, although it may have been anticipated by Baudelaire who wrote that 'the observer is a prince who enjoys his incognito everywhere'.[76]

Garance, in turn, hands over the role of observer to a similarly ambiguous figure, Lacenaire's accomplice and acolyte Avril, whose role consists almost entirely of looking and admiring. Avril listens to Lacenaire reading out the letter to the estranged husband; on Lacenaire's behalf he throws Baptiste out of the Rouge-gorge; at Lacenaire's invitation he hides behind the screen in Frédérick's dressing-room – he is, it turns out, the actor's greatest admirer and longs to meet him – to witness Lacenaire's seductive or murderous encounter with the actor. This, however, is merely a dry run for the scene of Lacenaire's bloodiest and literally most spectacular crime in the Turkish baths where he murders Montray, a crime which is entirely presented through Avril's voyeuristic reactions.

Carné's version of *Le Bain turc*

Like Garance, Avril is a figure of inversion. He is feminised by Fabien Loris's simpering performance and by markers such as the rose he wears behind his ear when approaching Baptiste in the Rouge-gorge. It is through Avril that, in keeping with his historical model, Lacenaire's homosexuality is intimated, initially in the Rouge-gorge and subsequently in Frédérick's dressing-room when Frédérick opens a bottle of champagne which erupts in a phallic spray. This scene, in which Lacenaire had destined Frédérick as the victim had the latter not given him money, is later consummated in the Turkish baths, with Montray as the victim of Lacenaire's evil designs. The baths, peopled by men whom we glimpse in various states of undress as Lacenaire, Avril in tow, strides through in search of his prey, are a fiction of Trauner's imagination as we have seen. But they may also be a covertly homosexual version of Ingres's painting *Le Bain turc* which is crammed full of female nudes in a variety of extravagant poses, a final, bravado reference to the Ingres gag running through the film.

In the homosexual voyeur Avril, we are given the image of the film viewer, the passive, feminised witness of an inverted image of reality, the amalgamation of the erotic and the visual metaphors running through *Les Enfants du paradis*. It is an image supported not just by the constant inversion of triangular relations, but also by the reworking of cinema history which the film proposes. Since the bipartite structure of the film is understood as one of repetition and rehearsal, and since one half is, in some sense, the mirror image of the other, then the figure which best accounts for this relation is that of the camera obscura. Of all the many optical toys popularised in the 19th century, the camera obscura was the most widely disseminated because it was cheap and portable, and because it was one of the earliest means of viewing moving pictures. As a precursor of the cinema it joins the boulevard entertainments presented in the film. And as a form of cultural interpretation it was invoked by Marx to explain the workings of ideology as an inverted image of reality. For the camera obscura holds a mirror up to nature, as the novel was supposed to do, but unlike that of the novel the representation it offers is an inverted image of reality, the point of inversion being, in the optical diagrams, the point at which the sides of two triangles cross over.

THE WORLD TURNED UPSIDE DOWN

A film of this length, complexity and above all ambition, especially one made at such a crucial moment in the history of France, demands to be read politically. Yet the structure of the film, with its parallels, *mises en abyme*, repetitions and prefigurations, seems deliberately designed to inhibit linear or univocal interpretations. However seductive they may seem, attempts to read the film as an allegory based on an equivalence between characters or events in the film and in the 'real' world have never proved satisfactory. So how can we understand the politics of *Les Enfants du paradis* and the message it conveyed about occupied France?

Some clues are to be found in the film's title. It is undoubtedly a 'heritage film', a statement about the politics of culture inspired by the Vichy government's insistence that its project was as much cultural as political and economic.[77] Much of its political impact resides in the way it places popular culture centre-stage. These, *'enfants du paradis'*, these 'children' of 'paradise' of the title, are the popular audience, whose tastes were held, in the democratic and post-classical era ushered in by the Revolution, to be more noble than those of earlier aristocratic and bourgeois audiences, and whose authenticity is underwritten by the spontaneity and simplicity of its pleasures and responses, evoked from time to time in the film, especially by Garance.[78]

The Boulevard was the place where all audiences found something to their taste, and that was its strength. It undermined the social order not just by bringing all classes together, often under one roof, but also by encouraging dialogue and interaction, commentary and exchange between audience and actors. [79] Time and again, those who appear most obviously spectators positioned safely in boxes, become drawn into what is happening on stage. This is why Frédérick transgresses the boundaries between play and audience by simultaneously positioning himself in the role of Robert Macaire and in that of the common man as a commentator on the play.

In placing the rabble in the 'gods', or the *'paradis'*, the theatre inverted the class system of the external world. In this way the popular theatre also echoed an earlier, carnival tradition, which is represented in the film's closing scenes, wherein, for the space of the play or the fair, the realities of the social hierarchy are turned upside down, the rulers are mocked, and the underdogs reign supreme. It is, of course, not certain

The carnival overwhelms Baptiste

Vidor's *The Crowd* inspired Carné's carnival

that this tradition is truly radical or subversive. Some authorities argue that the medieval carnivals were occasions for letting off steam precisely so that the social order could be maintained. Conversely, other analysts, inspired by Bakhtin, would interpret carnival, with its emphasis on the scatological, the 'lower bodily stratum', as in itself a revolutionary inversion of the order of things, a testimony to the inherent vitality of popular culture and its capacity for radical intervention.[80]

But, by the kind of ellipsis Prévert adored, these *'enfants du paradis'* are also the *'enfant(s) de Par(ad)is'* celebrated by Victor Hugo in the shape of Gavroche in *Les Misérables* and depicted on the barricades in Delacroix's famous July Revolution painting of *Liberty Guiding the People*. The *'enfants de Paris'*, the street urchins who roamed Paris in ever greater numbers as the city expanded and industrialised in the early part of the 19th century were known not just as streetwise rascals but also for their radicalism. In a refinement or perversion of the Romantic interest in childhood, these urchins were simultaneously unsullied innocents and vanguard revolutionaries, leading the people where others might have feared to tread. In making a film about the *'enfants de Paris'*, Carné is not just celebrating popular taste but also the vitality of a revolutionary tradition which, for all that it was a cliché, had lost none of its emotive power.

In the political context of the Occupation the mere evocation of Paris, let alone a celebration of its cultural heritage, could be seen as subversive. By placing the people of Paris centre stage, *Les Enfants du paradis* opposes the provincialism of the Vichy regime and its attempts to substitute the 'orders' of pre-Revolutionary France for the social classes of industrial society. In a counter-cultural move the film suggests, through Baptiste, that popular art is sublime, through Garance, that prostitution is truth, and through Lacenaire, that history is farce.[81]

Like so many films of the Occupation, *Les Enfants du paradis* is an escapist fantasy, in which the characters would rather hold on to their dreams than subscribe to the interpretations offered by Jéricho, a work of the imagination whose inward-looking and repetitive structure is profoundly solipsistic. It is also a magnificent artefact, a film about heritage which time has transformed into a monument marking the end of successful large-scale studio productions and of the period when French cinema could legitimately entertain universal pretensions. But perhaps the most positive message of the film derives from its inversions

of gender, genre and class. These provide the essential link which allows
the visual to be understood politically and transgression to be seen as a
more creative and radical act than opposition or resistance. At the end of
the film, when Garance leaves, the spirit of carnival overwhelms Baptiste
with its promise that in due course everything will return to 'normal',
and it is perhaps the knowledge of this lost opportunity, the failure of
carnival to perpetuate its inversions, which is the clue to the pathos of
Les Enfants du paradis.

NOTES

. . . .

1 See e.g. *Studio Magazine* 65, September 1992, p. 82.

2 See *L'Avant-scène cinéma* 72–73 (July–Sept. 1967), pp. 106–108.

3 Jean-Louis Barrault, *Souvenirs pour demain* (Paris: Editions du seuil, 1972), p. 167; Marcel Carné, *La Vie à belles dents* (Paris: Belfond, 1989), pp. 158–9.

4 Jean-Pierre Jeancolas, *Quinze ans d'années trente* (Paris: Stock, 1983), pp. 327–8; Jean-Pierre Bertin-Maghit, *Le Cinéma français sous l'Occupation* (Paris: Olivier Orban, 1989), p. 144.

5 Jean-Pierre Bertin-Maghit, *Le Cinéma français sous Vichy* (Paris: Albatros, 1980) p. 103.

6 Quoted in Bertin-Maghit, *Le Cinéma français sous l'Occupation*, p. 23.

7 See François Garçon 'Ce curieux âge d'or du cinéma français', in Jean Pierre Rioux (ed.), *La Vie culturelle sous Vichy* (Paris: Editions complexe, 1990), pp. 293–313. It is only a paradox in terms of the difficulties of supply. As far as organisation is concerned, it is clear that the war was the best thing that could have happened to the industry.

8 Marcel L'Herbier, *La Tête qui me tourne* (Paris: Belfond, 1979), p. 283.

9 After they invaded France in 1940 the Germans occupied the northern part of the country leaving the Vichy government jurisdiction over the southern part until 1943 when they occupied the remainder.

10 See Jean A. Gili, 'Cinecittà au secours du cinéma français', *Film Echange* vol. 38 no. 2 (1987), pp. 31–8.

11 For details of Paulvé's career during the war see Bertin-Maghit, *Le Cinéma français sous l'Occupation*, pp. 304–5.

12 For details of Paulvé's acquisition of La Victorine see Gili, 'Cinecittà …', p. 35.

13 See Jean A. Gili, 'La Vie cinémato-graphique à Nice de 1939 à 1945', *Annales de la Faculté des Lettres et des Sciences Humaines de Nice* 19 (1973), pp. 173–96.

14 See Roger Régent, *Cinéma de France sous l'Occupation* (Paris: Les Introuvables, 1975), pp. 90–94. The book was first published 1948.

15 Quoted in Gili, 'Cinecittà …', p. 32.

16 *L'Avant-scène cinéma*, p. 9.

17 Op. cit. p. 10

18 Marcel Carné and Jacques Prévert, *Les Enfants du paradis* (Paris: Balland, 1974).

19 Roger Leenhardt, 'Esthétique de Jacques Prévert', *Fontaine* 42 (May 1945), pp. 290–96.

20 He went to Hollywood after the war, made several notable films with Wilder, worked with Welles, and returned to France in his old age. But none of his subsequent sets was as ambitious as that of *Les Enfants du paradis*.

21 Carné, *La Vie à belles dents*, pp. 157–75.

22 See Jacques Hillairet, *Dictionnaire historique des rues de Paris*, 2 Vols (Paris: Editions de Minuit, 1963).

23 Bernard Marchand, *Paris, histoire d'une ville* (Paris: Editions du Seuil, 1993), p. 45.

24 Ibid.

25 Alexandre Trauner, *Décors de cinéma: Entretiens avec Jean-Pierre Berthomé* (Paris: Jade-Flammarion, 1988), p. 22.

26 Op. cit. p. 23.

27 See Walter Benjamin, *Charles Baudelaire, a Lyric Poet in the Era of High Capitalism* (London: NLB, 1969), p. 18.

28 See Louis Chevalier, *Classes laborieuses et classes dangereuses à Paris pendant la première moitié du XIXe siècle* (Paris: Plon, 1958), especially the chapter on Victor Hugo.

29 See Adrian Rifkin, *Street Noises* (Manchester: Manchester University Press, 1993), pp. 34–6.

30 Laundresses, traditionally independently employed and independently minded women, are Prévert favourites – compare the laundress in Renoir's *Le Crime de Monsieur Lange*.

31 For Montmartre see Louis Chevalier, *Montmartre du plaisir et du crime* (Paris: Robert Laffont, 1980), especially Part Two.

32 See Victor Hugo, *Les Misérables* (Paris: Garnier, 1957), p. 692: 'Paris, centre, suburbs, circumference; that is the whole earth for these children. They never venture further, and can no more leave the Parisian atmosphere than a fish can live out of water.'

33 See, for example, Christopher Prend-ergast, *Paris-Spectacle* (Paris: Editions de la Réunion des Musées Nationaux, 1987), p. 9.

34 Francis Carco, quoted in Robert Chazal, *Marcel Carné*, p. 89.

35 See Bernard Comment, *Le XIXe siècle des panoramas* (Paris: Adam Biro, 1993), especially pp. 89–94

36 Parodied by Meerson, Trauner's master, in René Clair's film *A nous la liberté*.

37 See Edward Braun, *Meyerhold on Theatre* (London: Methuen, 1969). All subsequent Meyerhold quotations are from this text.

38 Op. cit. p. 134.

39 Op. cit. p. 122.

40 Op. cit. p. 134.

41 It is interesting that after extolling the 'principles' of the fairground booth, Meyerhold immediately launches into a diatribe against the 'cinematograph' which he accuses of belonging to a period with a 'total obsession with naturalism' (p. 134).

42 *Les Enfants du paradis*, pp. 85–6.

43 Reprinted as Lacenaire, *Mémoires et autres écrits*, ed. Jacques Simonelli (Paris: José Corti, 1991).

44 Carné, *La Vie à belles dents*, p. 55.

45 Interestingly, Carné reports (*La Vie à belles dents*, p. 160) that Paulvé, worried by the length of Carné's proposed film, asked if it could be shown 'in episodes'.

46 Baudelaire in 'Le Vin des chiffonniers' (the ragpickers' wine) refers to 'his subjects, informers'. For Lacenaire's remarks see *Les Enfants du paradis*, p. 102.

47 Peter Brooks, *The Melodramatic Imagination* (New Haven & London: Yale University Press, 1976), p. 210, quotes one source which calculated the total number of crimes committed on stage at this time as 132,902.

48 For details see J. de Jomaron (ed.), *Le Théâtre en France*, 2 vols (Paris: A. Colin, 1989), vol. 2.

49 Sometimes its takings were as low as 100 francs a night, whereas it cost about 1,400 francs a night to stage a show.

50 Brooks, *The Melodramatic Imagination*, p. 43, quotes Charles Nodier's remark that melodrama is 'the only popular tragedy befitting our age' and his consciousness that melodrama played a 'special role' 'in the

context of a post-sacred universe, specifically in the post-Revolutionary landscape'.

51 Tristan Rémy, *Jean-Gaspard Deburau* (Paris: L'Arche, 1954), p. 11.

52 Jules Janin, *Histoire du théâtre à quatre sous pour faire suite à l'histoire du Théâtre-Français*, 2 Vols (Paris: Charles Gosselin, 1832).

53 Quoted in Rémy, *Jean-Gaspard Deburau*, p. 11.

54 Théophile Gautier, *Souvenirs de théâtre, d'art et de critique* (Paris: Charpentier, 1883), pp. 55–67.

55 Gautier, *Souvenirs*, p. 55.

56 Op. cit. p. 56.

57 *Les Enfants du paradis*, p. 273.

58 Op.cit. p. 244. No doubt also a reference to the Prévert brothers' film *Souvenirs de Paris*.

59 *Les Enfants du paradis*, p. 262.

60 In conversation with Baptiste on the Barrière de Ménilmontant, Garance emphasises her gaiety 'je suis gaie comme un pinson' (I'm as happy as a skylark). It will be recalled that Musset's Mimi worked in a laundry, and that after she had pawned her only dress to help a friend in need, she appeared in the street wearing a curtain, rather as Garance dresses in a bedspread in the continuation of this same scene with Baptiste. See A. de Musset, *Oeuvres complètes en prose* (Paris: Gallimard, 1960), pp. 714–43. Though she shared a name, Murger's Mimi had a different fate but she became celebrated through Puccini's opera *La Bohème* (1896), and this reminiscence may, again, reinforce the *fin de siècle* atmosphere of parts of the film.

61 See Anne Freadman, 'Reading the Visual', *Framework* 30/31 (1986), p. 155.

62 In *L'Armée des ombres* it is stated that France will not be free until its inhabitants can watch *Gone with the Wind*.

63 Just as Scarlett uses the drawing room curtains to make a frock in which to seduce Rhett Butler, so Garance uses Madame Hermine's counterpane to make an improvised oriental dress in which to seduce Baptiste.

64 '*Gars*', of course, means 'bloke' or 'lad' in French.

65 *Les Enfants du paradis*, p. 81.
66 Op. cit. p. 131
67 See Joan Rivière, 'Womanliness as a masquerade', reprinted in Victor Burgin, James Donald and Cora Kaplan (eds), *Formations of Fantasy* (London: Methuen, 1986), pp. 35–44.
68 *Les Enfants du paradis*, p. 273.
69 See, for example, Turk, *Child of Paradise*, p. 273.
70 See Eve Kosofsky Sedgwick, *Between Men* (New York: Columbia University Press, 1985), pp. 21–7.
71 Op.cit. p. 21.
72 Viz: Part One: Garance – Frédérick / Baptiste; Garance – Lacenaire/Baptiste; Baptiste – Garance/Nathalie; Lacenaire Avril/Baptiste; Lacenaire – Garance/Avril. In the second part two further triangles are added: Garance – Montray/Lacenaire; Lacenaire – Frédérick/Montray. Freadman, 'Reading the Visual', interestingly emphasises how the triangular figure is echoed through the costume and framing of the film's erotic scenes.
73 Charles Baudelaire, *Petits poèmes en prose* (Paris: Garnier, 1962), pp. 57–61; 71–4.

74 Op. cit. p. 72, 'Hercules proud of the enormity of their limbs', 'dancers as beautiful as fairies or princesses [who] are leaping and prancing in the light of the street lamps.'
75 Rifkin, *Street Noises*, p. 103.
76 Charles Baudelaire, *Curiosités esthétiques: L'Art romantique* (Paris: Garnier, 1962), p. 463.
77 See Christian Faure, *Le Projet culturel de Vichy* (Lyon: Presses Universitaires de Lyon/ CNRS, 1989).
78 For example, when watching Baptiste in Frédérick's company she draws attention to the innocent laughter of the audience in the '*paradis*', a gaiety she once shared herself.
79 See Jacques Rancière, 'Good Times, or Pleasure at the Barriers', in Adrian Rifkin and Roger Thomas (eds.), *Voices of the People* (London: Routledge, 1987), pp. 45–94.
80 See Mikhail Bakhtin, *Rabelais and his World* (Cambridge, Mass.: MIT Press, 1968).
81 So that Lacenaire describes the scene when Garance and Baptiste embrace as 'a vaudeville, a farce [...] For example, when a king is cuckolded, it is a tragedy, a drama of infidelity [..] but when it's a poor devil like you or me, Monsieur de Montray [...] it's a burlesque comedy', *Les Enfants du paradis*, pp. 310–11.

CREDITS
....

Les Enfants du paradis
I. Le Boulevard du Crime
II. L'Homme blanc

France
1945
Production companies
Production Société
Nouvelle Pathé Cinéma
A Pathé Consortium
Cinéma presentation
Production Managers
Raymond Borderie,
Fred Orain
Unit Manager
Louis Théron
Director
Marcel Carné
Artistic assistant
Pierre Blondy
Screenplay/Dialogue
Jacques Prévert
Shooting script
Marcel Carné
Director of photography
Maurice Thiriet
[Camera operator
Robert Schneider]
Pantomimes
Georges Mouqué
[Pantomimes assistant
Gilles Margaritis]
Orchestra
La Société des
Concerts du Conservatoire
Conductor
Charles Münch
Editor
Henry Rust
[Assistant editor
Madeleine Bonin]
Art directors
Léon Barsacq
Raymond Gabutti
[Assistant art director
Robert Clavel]
Costumes
Mayo

[Makeup
Paule Dean]
Technical assistant
Bruno Tireux
Sound engineer
Robert Teisseire
[Sound mixer
Jacques Carrère]
**Clandestine
collaborators**
Alexandre Trauner
(art direction)
Joseph Kosma (music)

Arletty
Garance
Jean-Louis Barrault
Baptiste Debureau
Pierre Brasseur
Frédérick Lemaître
Pierre Renoir
Jéricho
Maria Casarès
Nathalie
Gaston Modot
Fil de Soie, blind beggar
Fabien Loris
Avril, Lacenaire's assistant
Marcel Pérès
Director of the 'Funambules'
Etienne Decroux
Anselme Debureau
Jane Marken
Madame Hermine
Marcelle Monthil
Marie
Louis Florencie
Policeman
Habib Benglia
*Arab attendant of Turkish
bath*
Rognoni
Director of 'Grand Théâtre'

Jacques Castelot
Georges, first dandy
Paul Frankeur
Police inspector
Albert Rémy
Scarpia Barrigni
Robert Dhéry
Celestin
Auguste Boverio
First author
Paul Demange
Second author
Louis Salou
Count Edouard de Montray
Marcel Herrand
Pierre-François Lacenaire
Léon Larive
*Stage doorman of the
'Funambules'*
Jean Gold
Second dandy
Guy Favières
Debt collector
Lucienne Vigier
First pretty girl
Gynette Quero
Second pretty girl
Gustave Hamilton
*Stage doorman of the
'Grand Théâtre'*
Jean Diener
Third author
Lucien Walter
Ticket seller
Jean-Pierre Delmon
Little Baptiste
Jean Lanier
Iago
Raphaël Patorni
Third dandy
Jeanne Dussol
Bearded woman
Marcel Melrac
Policeman

Henry de Livry
Public writer's customer
Jean Carmet
Inspector
Rivers Cadet
Middle class man
Michel Vadet
Germain Aeros
Gosselin
Max Dejean
Pierre Réal

Choisin
Paul Temps
Grégoire Chabas
Liote
Albert Broquie
Maurice Cartier
Roger Vincent
Joe Alex
Bilboquet
Gérard Blain
Lucienne Legrand
Madhyanah Foy

95mins/97mins

Credits checked by
Markku Salmi

The print of *Les Enfants
du paradis* was specially
produced for the 360 Classic
Feature Films Project from
material deposited in the
National Film and
Television Archive by
Academy Film Distributors.

BIBLIOGRAPHY

. . . .

Transcriptions

Les Enfants du paradis in *L'Avant-scène cinéma* 72–73 (July–Sept. 1967).

Les Enfants du Paradis: A Film by Marcel Carné, trans. Dinah Brooke (London: Lorrimer, 1968) [English translation of the above].

Marcel Carné and Jacques Prévert, *Les Enfants du paradis* (Paris: Balland, 1974).

Secondary Sources

Jean-Louis Barrault, *Souvenirs pour demain* (Paris: Editions du Seuil, 1967).

Charles Baudelaire, *Curiosités esthétiques. L'Art romantique* (Paris: Garnier, 1962).

Charles Baudelaire, *Petits poèmes en prose* (Paris: Garnier, 1962).

Jean-Pierre Bertin-Maghit, *Le Cinéma français sous Vichy* (Paris: Albatros, 1980).

Jean-Pierre Bertin-Maghit, *Le Cinéma français sous l'Occupation* (Paris: Olivier Orban, 1989).

Marcel Carné, *La Vie à belles dents* (Paris: Belfond, 1989).

Robert Chazal (ed.), *Marcel Carné* (Paris: Seghers, 1965).

Christian Faure, *Le Projet culturel de Vichy* (Lyon: Presses Universitaires de Lyon/CNRS, 1989).

Théophile Gautier, *Souvenirs de théâtre, d'art et de critique* (Paris: Charpentier, 1883).

Jules Janin, *Histoire du Théâtre à quatre sous pour faire suite à l'histoire du Théâtre-Français*, 2 Vols (Paris: Charles Gosselin, 1832).

Jean-Pierre Jeancolas, *Quinze ans d'années trente* (Paris: Stock, 1983).

René Jeanne and Charles Ford, *Paris vu par le cinéma* (Paris: Hachette, 1969); 'Le Paris de Marcel Carné', pp. 118-36.

Bernard Landry, *Marcel Carné* (Paris: Editions Jacques Vautrin, 1952).

Marcel L'Herbier, *La Tête qui me tourne* (Paris: Belfond, 1979).

Michel Pérez, *Les Films de Marcel Carné* (Paris: Ramsay, 1986).

Roger Régent, *Le Cinéma français sous l'Occupation* (Paris: Les Introuvables, 1975).

Tristan Rémy, *Jean-Gaspard Deburau* (Paris: L'Arche, 1954).

Adrian Rifkin, *Street Noises* (Manchester: Manchester University Press, 1993).

Jean-Pierre Rioux (ed.) *La Vie culturelle sous Vichy* (Paris: Editions complexe, 1990).

Geneviève Sellier, *Les Enfants du paradis. Etude critique* (Paris: Nathan, 1992).

Alexandre Trauner, *Décors de cinéma: Entretiens avec Jean-Pierre Berthomé* (Paris: Jade/Flammarion, 1988).

Edward Baron Turk, *Child of Paradise: Marcel Carné and the Golden Age of French Cinema* (Cambridge, Mass.: Harvard University Press, 1989).

Journals

Les Cahiers de la cinémathèque no. 5 (Winter 1972); 'Revoir Marcel Carné', pp. 2–59.

Anne Freadman, 'Reading the Visual', *Framework* 30/31 (1986), pp. 134-57.

'Jean A. Gili, 'Cinecittà au secours du cinéma français', in *Film Echange* vol. 38 no. 2 (1987) pp. 31-8.

Jean A. Gili, 'La Vie cinématographique à Nice de 1939 à 1945', in *Annales de la Faculté des Sciences Humaines de Nice* 19 (1973), pp. 173-96.

L'ATALANTE

....

Marina Warner

ALSO PUBLISHED

If you would like further information about future BFI Film Classics or about other books on film, media and popular culture from BFI Publishing, please write to:

BFI Film Classics
British Film Institute
21 Stephen Street
London
W1P 2LN